Exegeting the City

Exegeting the City

*What You Need to Know About Church Planting
in the City Today*

SEAN BENESH

Urban Loft Publishers | Portland, Oregon

Exegeting the City
What You Need to Know About Church Planting
in the City Today

Urban Loft Publishers
2034 NE 40th Avenue #414
Portland, OR 97212
www.urbanloftpublishers.com

ISBN: 978-0692589793

Made in the U.S.A.

To those who are creatively proclaiming and demonstrating
the Gospel in the city ...

Contents

Metrospiritual Book Series

In my first book, *Metrospiritual*, I was looking for a term or a way to define what an urban-centric approach to faith and Scripture looks like. This came about as I wrestled through how do we reconcile the urban trajectory of humanity throughout Scripture, the current state of rapid urbanization and globalization, along with where we'll spend eternity. Similarly, with the church still viewing life, faith and Scripture either through a rural or a suburban lens, I believe it is time for a new set of lenses. This is what I call *metrospiritual*. I define it as, "taking an urban lens to the reading, understanding, interpretation, and application of Scripture." The *Metrospiritual Book Series* explores various aspects, elements, ideas, and methodologies, and the theology of what an urban-centric faith looks like as expressed in the city. A *metrospirituality* can have a shaping effect on the way the church lives in, loves, serves, embraces, and engages the city with the Good News of the Kingdom of God.

Sean Benesh

Other Books in the Series

The Multi-Nucleated Church: Towards a Theoretical Framework for Church Planting in High-Density Cities (2015).

The Bikeable Church: A Bicyclist's Guide to Church Planting (2015).

Blueprints for a Just City: The Role of the Church in Urban Planning and Shaping the City's Built Environment (2015)

.

Preface

The question that the Preface attempts to answer is the *why* question. In other words, *why* was this book written? For me the answer to that question is very straightforward. I want church planters to not only wrestle through contextualization questions on the front end of planting, but to also begin developing a deeper understanding of cities.

Church planting in city centers continues to take off as more and more planters are flocking to the urban core. I had a recent conversation with a denominational church planting coach who oversees church planting in Chicago. While there are 2.7 million people within the city limits and another seven million in the suburbs, he told me that it is incredibly difficult to find someone interest in planting in the suburbs anymore. Every church planter now wants to plant in the city.

The same narrative is repeated in every major city across North America. Urban is *in* and suburbs is *out.* I see this all of the time here in Portland where I meet wave after wave of church planters moving to the heart of the city. When I travel to other cities and work with church planters the storyline remains the same. So I wrote a book for them. For you.

What I've come to learn is that most church planters don't come from other urban contexts. They are moving in from the suburbs, other small cities, or small towns. Most are not "citified." No worries though, because seemingly everyone else moving to cities is in the same boat so rest assured. We all develop our "street legs" soon enough.

However, the obvious is still true ... cities *are* different. Not just different from the suburbs, but different from the smaller cities or small towns that many church planters have moved from. But what do I mean by *different?* How different? And then for me then the next logical question is ... what are the ramification for church planting?

Urban density *does* matter. There's something magical that happens as cities become more dense and vertical. More than merely upping the amount of people per square mile (or kilometer) density does impact and change culture. What often times distinguishes the city center from the suburbs? Density. However it is *much more* than that.

How much is *much more?* That is what this book is about. This is for those of you who are venturing into the city for the first time to plant. Maybe you're too smug, confident, or cocky to admit that you really don't know all that much about the city. A podcast here, a Keller book there, and you think you're set. But I want to assure you that this is a safe place to let your guard down. Come in as a learner. Expand your understanding of the city to aid you in the process of contextualizing not only *how* you're going to plant a church, but how you're going to teach and proclaim the Gospel.

Besides ... your city needs you to do this. Your city needs Christ. Check your ego at the door and come and learn.

Acknowledgements

The last seven books that I've written (including this one) have gone through the refining process of my good friend Frank Stirk. He has probably now spent hundreds (and hundreds) of hours scrutinizing my every word in order to help me communicate the message that I'm wanting to get out. Thank you! Thank you for your patience, faithfulness, long-suffering, hard work, diligence, kindness, and friendship. I couldn't have done this without you.

Exegeting the City

Introduction

This semester at Warner Pacific College here in Portland I am teaching a course called *History of the American City*. Stepping away from the usual urban ministry or church planting courses that I have been teaching the last number of years, this class is a bona fide history class ... of the American city no less. One of our textbooks details the history of Portland from its tentative start to its growth into the city that it is today. History truly is a great teacher.

While we started of in the course looking at the establishment of colonial outposts on the eastern seaboard that grew into cities of significant size and influence like New York or Boston, one of the constant reminders is the evolving or changing form or structure of our cities as well as the change in culture as wave after wave of immigrants have shaped and reshaped the United States. We *are* truly a nation of immigrants.

In fact, one of the common narratives of the city is simply this ... *change*. As our nation transitioned from an agricultural-based economy to industrial and then post-industrial economy, each of these changes impacted not only urban form but also urban culture. Overlying these are the changes in transportation technologies from walking to horse-powered streetcars to electric streetcars to automobiles and again, each change has impacted not only urban form but urban culture as well. And then on top of that are the changing technologies that keep reorienting our lives.

Such is the world that today's city church planters have to contend with. As they strive to successfully launch a new church *ex nihilo* they will hopefully in the process rely on solid missiology and skilled cultural exegesis. For the uninitiated, exegesis is simply "an explanation or critical interpretation of a text." Scholars and theologians pull apart texts, both biblical and literary classics, sift through them, conduct word studies, look at the field of meaning of those words, their historical usages and so on, and then put them back together again in a way that provides the text with a more robust and deeper meaning. That same skill can be applied to cities.

The text of the city is its culture. It is more than skyscrapers, transit lines, freeways, strip malls, or single family detached homes. It is the text that reveals the values and worldviews of its citizens. As with a historical text we need to apply exegetical skills to the city. We need to analyze it, sift through it, pull it apart, and ultimately put it back together in such a way that it provides us with a deeper, more well-rounded, and more accurate view and understanding of our cities. Seminarians have become skilled at exegeting biblical texts, but how have church planters fared with our cities?

More than likely you picked up this book because you care about cities, are interested in cities, and/or want to develop a better understanding of them. You have a desire to know how to exegete your city or at least discover some of the trends impacting urban life today since it has a direct impact upon church planting specifically and ministry in general. This book is simply about noting the trends and changes that are reshaping North American cities. It is my hope that after reading this you'll have a better handle or grasp on some of the changing realities taking place in your city. Various trends get an earlier start in some cities before they happen in others. As I travel to more and more cities in the US and Canada, I get a first hand look at these changes and I can almost plot them out on a continuum that tracks where they are in relation to the topics that we'll be looking at.

My motivation in writing this book is to share *some* of the changes that cities are undergoing which are reorienting how we not only view cities but live in them as well. The topics before you may be felt more acutely in some cities or neighborhoods than in others. In this regard, this book is simply an *aid* as an exegetical tool. The actual work on the ground can only be done by *you* in *your* city. All I can do is try to stimulate your thinking and to point out how our cities are changing. Lastly, these are topics that are near and dear to me as they deal with what impacts urban form which in turn influences how we do ministry in the city. There are more topics that are not addressed than are addressed.

I wish you the best as you learn to exegete your cities for the furtherance of the Gospel and the planting of new churches.

Exegeting the City

Chapter 1

Tools for Exegeting the City

Along with teaching at Warner Pacific College, over the past several semesters I have also taught classes at North Portland Bible College. Last week we wrapped up the semester where I taught *Church Planting in an Urban Context*. The school was formed when the neighborhoods of inner North and Northeast Portland were primarily African-American. Since then the school has been intrinsically linked to the area's black churches and leaders. My class was comprised entirely of African-Americans, several of whom are currently pastors in churches in the neighborhood.

I tell you that because of this ... there would seemingly be a lot of assumptions or common ideas of what "church planting in an urban context" should or should not look like based upon the school's rich history and the cultural and ethnic make-up of my class. However, my goal for that class was to redefine what "urban" really means for the twenty-first century city. In that regard, we spent considerable class time discussing how to exegete cities, looking at population density and urban form. Our class exercises focused on international urban centers like Dubai, Tokyo, Vancouver (Canada), and so on. These experiences and exercises led us to create an urban immersion class where we would spend three to four days up in Vancouver doing what we just finished studying in class.

Now why did I do that? The students in my class were from varying backgrounds. For example, some had been born and raised in the projects in Boston. So it would seem that they would have (or at least *should have*) a common understanding of what "urban" really means and what it's all about. Instead, we spent our field experiences in Portland doing such things as riding the streetcar through the Pearl District, walking around South Waterfront which sits on the southern edge of the central business district, and exploring the Jade District which is our Asian district centered around 82nd and Division. What we had thought or assumed was "urban" all of a sudden came into question.

This was highlighted during one of our classroom exercises where the students role-played as a core group and had to create strategies to plant a church in Dubai. It became evident that what we may mean by "urban" doesn't really apply outside of our borders, whether in Dubai or the slums of Mumbai or Mexico City. Words are moving targets. Their definitions can be transitory. We cannot simply default to past definitions. We cannot assume that cities are static and that once we "figure them out" then our work is done.

What really clicked for these leaders who pastor churches in rapidly gentrifying neighborhoods was that they are truly cross-cultural missionaries who had never left home. Instead the neighborhood around them is changing and at an incredibly fast pace. The major corridors in their neighborhood are densifying and becoming vertical, going from lower density single family detached homes to buildings that are four-to-six stories tall. And that's creating a cultural shift, because the people moving in are significantly different from those who lived there even fifteen years ago. "Urban" is a moving target.

Rather than becoming preoccupied with what "urban" means or at least how that term came to be connected with words like "ministry" or "church," the purpose of the class was instead on how to exegete our cities today. For this group the goal was to expand on and redefine what "urban" even means. It was also to show them what else "urban" is and could be here in Portland. What do we even mean by "urban Portland?"

One night as we walked downtown around the north end of the Pearl District and its sleek new residential towers we addressed and discussed what it would take to plant a church in this highly urban neighborhood. It was a different kind of "urban" than these men from inner-city neighborhoods of the 1980s were used to. The neighborhood before us was new, affluent, and comprised of mostly ethnic whites. So what then is "urban?"

But you see, that is the wrong question to begin with (even though I was the one who asked it). Rather than talking about what is or is not "urban," we instead need to instead talk things such as changing urban morphology, contextualization, exegeting cities, and the like. When it comes to understanding our cities or exegeting them it is almost like we need to jettison terms and definitions and simply start from scratch. And if we did so ... where would we even begin?

Contextualization

The place to begin exegeting the city is contextualization.[1] So what is it and what does it mean in relation to church planting?

Contextualization—The dynamic process whereby the constant message of the gospel interacts with specific, relative human situations. It involves an examination of the gospel in the light of the respondent's worldview and then adapting the message, encoding it in such a way that it can become meaningful to the respondent.

good def

Contextual Church Planting—Attempts to communicate the Gospel in word and deed and to establish churches in ways to make sense to people within their local cultural context. It is primarily concerned with presenting Christianity in such a way that it meets peoples' deepest needs and penetrates their worldviews, thus allowing them to follow Christ and remain in their own cultures.[2]

also good

What we can see from these definitions is that contextualization is the fluid and dynamic process of the Gospel interacting with culture. Each time that takes place it involves a translation on some level whether linguistic,

---

[1] One of the best resources for contextualization is *Center Church* by Timothy Keller. His chapters on contextualization represent some of the best material out there on the subject. I used this book for the course textbook in my *Church Planting in an Urban Context* class. The students *loved* this book.

[2] Frost and Hirsch, *The Shaping of Things to Come*, 83.

cultural, or worldview. Bosch reminds us that "The Christian faith never exists except as 'translated' into culture."[3]

This idea of "translated into culture" seems obvious when we envision an international setting where the language and culture are foreign to our home culture. However, as I pointed out in the examples earlier in this chapter with my class, this translation or contextualization process *must happen* even in our cities and that the process differs from district to district. To plant a church in the Pearl District would differ contextually from the Jade District. Not only that, but the same applies if we planted a church in the Hollywood District or Goose Hollow or Alberta Arts District. And these examples are all merely from a seemingly homogenous city like Portland.

Caleb Crider in *Tradecraft* writes, "For the sake of mission, contextualization means adjusting how we communicate the gospel so that people do not need to join a new culture in order to hear and understand the message."[4] We seem to have this nailed when we travel *over there*, but so often we fail to walk through that same process *over here*. Why so? That was my motive for taking my class and exposing them to different cultural settings that are here in Portland that fall under the label of "urban." To call something "urban" is not a monocultural label that applies to all cities let alone to all parts of the same city like Portland.

Even in the downtown core the students became aware of how different the cultural realities were in comparing the Pearl

---

[3] Bosch, *Transforming Mission,* 447.

[4] McCrary, et al., *Tradecraft,* 148.

with Nob Hill or the area around Portland State University or South Waterfront. On our streetcar tour we noticed immediately once we drew close to the university that all of a sudden the people who hopped onboard were mostly internationals. Another observation that we talked about as a class was why were there no other African-Americans on the streetcar.

So where is the starting line?

In our class I laid out several examples to work through. For this exercise, the entire class acted as a church planting core team. We looked initially at three different cities ... Manchester (UK), Tucson (AZ), and Dubai (UAE). For each scenario I asked the class, "Let's say you're mobilizing a church planting team to start a new church ... where would you start once you land?" Initially the responses were similar to church planting strategies that are the norm across the continent (even though Tucson was an example from the US): We'd gather a core, figure out marketing strategies, look for a space to rent, entice people to come and hear a preacher, and so on. However, with each answer I pushed back. I asked them, "Would a missionary do that?"

You see, in supposedly culturally "familiar" places such as the UK or even Tucson, there seems to be the common assumption that church planting is already a signed, sealed and delivered packaged deal. All we need to do is follow the same recipe as everyone else, add water, and shake vigorously. But once we started talking about Dubai or later on Tokyo then the rules all of a sudden began to change. No sandwich board signs, no focusing on creating a hip gathering for convinced worshippers, no slick marketing, and so many other things we *assume* is the norm for church planting. Why the change?

Contextualization.

But ... shouldn't we be doing that *here* in North America as well? Yes. But this is where we've become lazy missiologists in that we don't seem to work through those same processes here on our home turf. Why is that? Maybe some illustrations may help.

Manufactured vs. Custom Homes

Too often church planting resembles manufactured homes. Manufactured homes are created in warehouses or manufacturing sites divorced from where they will eventually be delivered. Suppose these homes are built in a suburb of Detroit. Once constructed they will then be placed on a flatbed trailer and hauled to their location whether Arkansas, Arizona, Nebraska, or Kentucky. Same house and same style regardless of the location. These homes do not take into account the local nuances of culture, common building materials, climate, local or regional architecture styles, and so on. Same house and same style regardless of location. Design is divorced from context.

Church planting can look that way. We pile into conferences where those on the big stage are those in whom our church and church planting subculture have deemed "successful" since *they* grew their churches large through visionary leadership and strategy. While church planters who attend these conferences are not explicitly told this, these speakers serve as examples for the template that we're encouraged to adopt whether consciously or subconsciously. These become akin to manufactured homes. Or church planting training systems become like the warehouse that's cranking out manufactured homes: They are void of context. The workers simply follow cookie cutter blueprints and procedures.

I have been through too many training sessions for church planters that felt like I was being told to swing a hammer on an assembly line because all we're doing is prefabricating one-size-fits-all homes regardless if one plants in Brooklyn or Boston or Tulsa or Fort Worth. So what is the alternative?

Custom homes.

In contrast custom homes are built on site. They factor in such things as climate, local and regional culture and architectural styles, local building materials, local skilled workers, and the like. You see, a home in the foothills of Tucson in the arid Sonoran Desert needs to be significantly different from a home in the wet climate of Portland or Seattle in the Pacific Northwest. There is a big difference between planning for eights months of summer temps or eight months of rain. Custom homes are adapted to and shaped by local culture.

A custom home in the Sonoran Desert will use either stucco or adobe, the color palette will make sure that the home blends into the natural desert surroundings, and double-pane windows and tile floors will be added to keep the house cool in the summer. Manufactured homes built in a climate-controlled building in Michigan do not take regional and climate differences into account. All one needs to do is scrape a clearing and plop the house on the lot. No contextualization is needed.

Contextualization and History

Let's be honest up front and admit that since the birth of the church we have struggled greatly to live in this tension of contextualizing not only the Gospel but also the forms or expressions of church. While we today have the luxury of seeing everything in hindsight, the reality is that our forefathers did the best that they knew how. But without a shadow of doubt the church has been enculturating[5] since its inception and will always do so.

As a quick example, I'm writing this just before Easter. It is the high-water mark of our annual church calendar and the foundation of what it means to be a Christian ... but how did we even come up with the name? Philip Jenkins notes, "In the English language, even the greatest Christian festival, Easter, bears the name of a pagan spring goddess."[6] So for the most important Christian celebration we co-opted the name from pagan religion. Contextualization. Enculturation. Adaptation. From the beginning we have been sifting through what to keep in culture, what to redeem, and what to jettison. Let's explore in brief some of these.

The early church struggled with translation into the Greco-Roman world. Culturally it was akin to a salmon transitioning from fresh water to salt water. The "cultural water" in the Judaic world was *significantly* different than that

---

[5] "The process whereby individuals learn their group's culture, through experience, observation, and instruction." Dictionary.com, Inc. "Enculturation."

[6] Jenkins, *The Next Christendom*, 129.

of the Gentile world. Worldviews differed greatly. Monotheism came up against polytheism. The Gospel and the church had to make a significant cultural leap. What we find then in the letters of Paul are the struggles involved in making this translation. It was messy. No more visiting the temple prostitutes. No more worshipping hand-crafted idols. No more sacrificing meat to idols. No more sexual promiscuity. In each letter Paul called the people back to the Gospel and their new identity in Christ which embraced all cultures and ethnicities. This was the tenor of the Jerusalem Council in Acts 15. David Bosch reminds us that:

> After AD 85 Judaism had to distinguish itself clearly not only from paganism but also from the church. Similarly, Christians had to battle on two fronts: against the synagogue and against Hellenistic religions. In its early stages, Christianity was undoubtedly closer to Judaism; in its later stages it would, in many respects, be closer to the Greek milieu, in spite of initial resistance from theologians such as Tatian (110-180 A.D.) and Tertullian (155-222 A.D.). The shift already becomes discernible in the terminology used. Concepts originally typical of the cult of the emperor, the military, the Greek mystery religions, the theater, and Platonic philosophy gradually became common in Christian worship and doctrine.[7]

As the church throughout Acts and for the first few centuries shifted from the Jewish world to the Gentile world it formed the basis of our identity. The Gospel was not confined to one culture or ethnicity. From the beginning it was urban and multicultural. "The early church, 'in straddling the Jewish-

---

[7] *Transforming Mission*, 192.

Gentile worlds, was born in a cross-cultural milieu with translation as its birthmark.' It should therefore come as no surprise that in the Pauline churches Jews, Greeks, barbarians, Thracians, Egyptians, and Romans were able to feel at home."[8]

Sometimes I am asked why or how we connected with the church that we are a part of here in Portland. Surprisingly the answer and reasoning are more subconscious than anything else. As the above quote suggests, the church that we are connected with feels like home in the sense that it has a cultural affinity with Portland. When we host our home community or walk into the building for worship celebrations on Sundays there is no stepping into a time warp or into a culture or ethos that differs from the surrounding neighborhood and city. The church reflects the neighborhood and city well. It has enculturated, adapted, and translated.

So what does this process look like?

Missiological Stating Point

The first realization is that God is and has been at work here in our cities long before we showed up.

> To believe in prevenient grace is to assume that God goes before us even into the most irreligious situations and creates fields or environments in which our Christlike example can be received. Exiles acknowledge that. They go confidently into the world on the assumption that God goes beforehand. Our job, then, is not to make things happen, but to cooperate with God, who is already making them happen.[9]

---

[8] Ibid., 448.

[9] Frost, *Exiles*, 142.

What does that quote say to you? How does it apply to contextual church planting? Living in the Pacific Northwest I have seen the national narrative on church planting play out over and over again. Here is what I mean. For those outside of Oregon, Washington, or British Columbia the common storyline is this idea that this is a "pre-Christian" region. In other words, there is this pervasive myth in church planting circles that the cities up here have never had a Gospel or church presence. So the term pre-Christian is used. While it sounds catchy, it is simply untrue.

The reality is that the church has always had a presence here. The great history book *Portland In Three Centuries* by local urban historian Carl Abbott even details how early church leaders were instrumental in advocating for justice and equity in Portland. In other words, these local pastors were also influential in shaping the city. God has been at work everywhere since the beginning and continues to be at work up through today. That forms then our missiological starting point ... God is already *here*.

Foundations for Contextualization

While this is true we also need to learn to discern and dissect culture, extract vital information, and interpret the cultural narrative. Kevin Vanhoozer gives us three principles of ways to study culture:

- A HERMENEUTICAL principle: an attention to lived experience, especially that of the poor, as the medium in which biblical interpretation takes place.

2 • A CRITICAL principle: an analysis of social structures and a praxis oriented to liberating transformation.

3 • A CULTURAL principle: an attempt to make use of indigenous categories in order to convert people to Christ without destroying their memories and cultural identities.[10]

While this list details "a formal and a material insight that provides some methodological common ground between various third world theologies,"[11] it applies to the process of contextualization. Frost and Hirsch offer more insights into a critical contextualization of the Gospel:

- Examine closely the host culture.
- Maintain a clear commitment to biblical authority.
- People in the host culture are to critically evaluate their own past customs in light of their new biblical understandings, and to make decisions regarding their response to their newfound faith.[12]

The challenge with critical contextualization is that as culture-bound beings we both intentionally and unintentionally import our own culture into whatever context we are ministering in. It was my intention my *Church Planting in an Urban Context* class to shake things up since the term "urban" is a culturally conditioned term. It means one thing in Brooklyn and another thing in Portland and another thing in

---

[10] Vanhoozer, "One Rule to Rule Them All?" 98.

[11] Ibid.

[12] *The Shaping of Things to Come*, 89.

Mexico City and still another thing in Dubai. Through our contextualization exercise of role playing that we were planting a church in Dubai, we learned that we simply couldn't operate there as we would if we were church planting here in Portland. Why? Context. What is needed? Translation.

Wilbert R. Shenk in *Globalizing Theology* points out, "From the human point of view, there is no way we can engage with the gospel independent of culture. Our interaction with the gospel relies on human language, worldview, and cultural context."[13] It is through this study of culture that we not only learn to contextualize and translate the Gospel, but also the forms and expressions of church. You see, there is no universal approach to how churches function and operate because learning and teaching styles, music, and community differ greatly from culture to culture.

The challenge before us is to truly do the hard work of contextualization and not simply import church culture as we know it in our home context. "As is often the case in external diffusion, foreigners tend to reproduce their original culture in the new culture. In other words, the behavior and ideas of the missionaries reflect to a larger extent the state of their native culture at the moment when they left it."[14] That nails the biggest challenges of church planting when it comes to contextualization. Most often we are lazy at this, particularly when it comes to planting on the home soil of North America. I know because I failed at this as well.

---

13 Shenk, "Foreword," 9.

14 Uhalley Jr. and Wu, *China and Christianity*, 91.

When I ventured into my first church planting experience I didn't do anything remotely close to working through contextualization. In fact, I lived a state away from where we ended up planting. I created our church name, branding, strategy, and so on *before* we even moved to the city where we planted. When asked how we were going to plant or what our culture or church vibe was going to be like my answer was, "We're doing a Willow Creek / Saddleback hybrid."

Fortunately after six months of living in our new city I ended up jettisoning everything I had planned and strategized while living fifteen hundred miles away. We were forced to *begin* contextualizing (although I never knew of the term) on the fly which was fun, adventuresome, and exciting. It completely changed how I viewed church, church planting, cities, culture, and the like. Later on when I became a church planting strategist I would tell planters moving to our city *not* to name their church, create strategies, or start branding or do anything like that until they lived here for at least a year. Every city and region in North America is so unique that those coming in from outside need to spend time grounding and rooting themselves in the city first. But even then, culture is in flux.

Do supporters allow for this?

"Cultures are restless and dynamic. They rise and fall—flourishing for a time and then stagnating or disintegrating. New cultures arise to replace those that have disappeared."[15] This then leads into tackling and wrestling with some contextual foundations that will aid in church planting. Here are some points to keep in mind:

---

[15] *Globalizing Theology*, 9.

- All cultures are sinful and fallen and cloud all human understanding of God's revelation.
- All cultures have some degree of general revelation or prevenient grace whereby certain aspects of God's revelation in Jesus Christ may be clearly understood.
- All Christians must necessarily be incarnated into a culture.
- No one expression of church has a complete grasp of the host culture; contextualization is therefore this dynamic process of translated God, theology, and the church in context.[16]

Frost and Hirsch offer more insight into this contextualization process:

- Keep that which is not unbiblical—Many cultural practices are neither Christian nor non-Christian. They are neither sanctioned nor condemned in the Bible, and therefore Christians can be ambivalent about them.
- Reject that which is unbecoming for Christians.
- Modify practices to give them explicitly Christian meaning.
- Reject current unbiblical practices and replace them.
- Adopt rites drawn from the Christian heritage.
- Create new symbols and rituals.[17]

As a class exercise we looked at different groups of people and discussed and strategized what it would entail to plant churches among them. Since my class was made up of ethnic black Americans I tried to come up with groups different from them. Here was one of the examples:

---

16 Van Engen, "The Glocal Church," 179.

17 *The Shaping of Things to Come*, 90.

34

Sub-Culture #1

The center of life seems to revolve around a several city block radius full of coffee shops, bars, restaurants, shops, art galleries, and other oddities. This group is not part of the city's mainstream and for the most part it is a semi-close knit group of people who share the common interest in this part of the city, the eclectic nature of their group and setting, and an unspoken understood set of underlying values. Most didn't grow up in that area but for whatever reason in their adulthood were drawn to it. Maybe it was the university life close by, a burgeoning art scene, the liberal political bent of the people and area, freedom of lifestyle or sexual orientation, and so on.

These people would consider themselves as very spiritual but are extremely skeptical of organized or institutional religions especially Christianity. Claiming the church is too hypocritical and aligned with the Republican Party (which they detest) they would not go near a church at all and have only disdain for it. Sitting in a café with these people you'll hear occasional stories of growing up in the church and even cases of being abused or exploited. What they long for is a spirituality that works. One that makes this world a better place, takes care of people and puts them first, is tolerant and respectful of all religions, and one that sees the environment and its care a spiritual issue.

The irony of this example is that it generically represents Portland and even the changing dynamics of the specific neighborhoods that these pastors minister in. You see, when they each began leading their churches the neighborhoods were still predominantly black and comprised the heart of the African-American community here in Portland. Around 2000 the first shock waves of gentrification began to be felt. As the

2000s moved along the pace of gentrification and neighborhood succession began to pick up pace. Now these neighborhoods house a dwindling African-American population where they are no longer the majority.

The "a-ha" moment from this example and exercise for these church leaders was the realization that they are now ministering in a cross-cultural setting. In other words, it is essential for them to *not* think like a pastor of a church as much as it *is* to begin thinking like an international missionary ... except they had never moved away. The neighborhood around them had changed.

Missional Ecclesiology

Where do you start first? With the form or expression of the church or with the people? When church planters they tell me about their church planting efforts the conversation quickly moves towards their Sunday gatherings, the ethos or vibe of the worship setting, how they preach (and how long), music styles, stage design, and so on. Should that even be the starting point? Too often church planters want to hurry through the contextualization process (if they actually do it at all) to get to their bread and butter ... preaching. Why is that?

There is nothing wrong with preaching. In fact, solid biblical teaching is foundational for the health and growth of the church. Paul in his epistles continuously called the church to sound doctrine. I don't minimize good theology and sound biblical teaching by any stretch. I would even place myself theologically in the Reformed camp which has the reputation of a high commitment to orthodoxy. But I don't think that's the reason church planters want to quickly get to the public gathering stage so they can preach, have trendy worship gatherings for the convinced, and create cool stage backdrops.

If the starting point in church planting is contextualization church planters face the frightening reality that after the process is complete, the life of the church, its expression, and how it gathers may look nothing like what they had in mind going in. The challenge is this: most of us have the end goal of the gathering in mind long before we start the contextualization process ... *if* a planter even walks through the process.

As staff members, we may be frustrated with the uncouth manner in which our church handles worship and teaching at the Sunday gathering. Out of frustration we envision planting a church that *we* would really like to be a part of. Ironically though, the church expression that was cool in the 1990s was not cool in the early 2000s, and now what was cool even in 2005 is no longer cool (like a soul patch). In other words, your cool and hip worship gathering will soon become unhip and uncool just like the church you're trying to get away from. Rarely do churches continue the contextualization process even after they've begun.

Several years ago Ed Stetzer made a statement that is as true today as it was when he wrote these words: "Most church planters start the church in their head and not in their community. They come with preconceived notions, things they have always wanted to try, and strategies they were never allowed to use. This may make the planter relate better to the church, but the planter is called to reach the community. That requires planting a church into community, a church that is indigenous."[18] The follow-up question then is: How do you ensure an indigenous expression of church? What does that even look like? It goes back to contextualization. Stetzer continues, "But a truly indigenous church seeks to become incarnate within the culture in which it finds itself."[19]

There are some initial questions that we *must* wrestle with as we figure out what an indigenous adaptation of church looks like. Each question will send us on a journey that forces us into deeper theological reflection.

- What is your definition of church?
- Was the book of Acts and Epistles *prescriptive* or *descriptive* when it comes to church?
- How much are we allowed to "tinker with" when it comes to expressions of church? How much of the expression or forms of "church" that we find in the New Testament culturally bound? How much was reactionary? Or was the way it was done then a universal biblical truth for all times and cultures? How do you decide what to keep and what to discard?

Along with those questions, here are more questions to ask when you engage a new host culture with a view to planting a church:

- Who are these people? What is their past? What is their story? How did they get here? What are they like? What are their hopes, their dreams, their future goals?

---

[18] Stetzer, *Planting Missional Churches*, 29-30.

[19] Ibid., 30.

- How do you become an insider?
- What is their view of God and/or spiritual things?
- Where do you see God already at work?
- How would you go about engaging them with the Gospel? How will you teach them about God?
- What do you do if people respond to the Gospel and begin the journey of following God?
- How much of a non-contextualized Christianity will you import from your own host culture? How do you ensure that the new church is biblically faithful as well as a contextualized expression?
- What other questions should do you ask?

Contextualization is a tough and messy job! The good news is that you're not alone. The luxury you have with the internet, rapid travel, and communication is that you can network with others who are doing the same thing all over the world. You can cross-check with others in your sub-culture, your city, or region to help ensure you're planting a biblically faithful indigenous church. It was messy and difficult in the first century, it was messy throughout church history, and it still is today. But we should also see in that the freedom to engage in this wrestling, this work hard, of exegeting Scripture, exegeting culture, and then strategize accordingly.

The following chapters represent several trends that are reshaping cities in North America. As we contextualize and exegete our cities we need to be aware of some of the movements that are recalibrating the way we live in and experience them. Think of the following chapters as exegetical tools or insights as you work through exegeting your particular city. Some of these topics will apply more acutely in some cities more than others, but they are significantly impacting life of urbanites in North America (and globally).

Chapter 2

Urban Revitalization and Mission to the City

Inner-city Portland certainly lives up to its reputation as a cool, hip, trendy, bohemian enclave. This morning as I sit in Heart Coffee at one of the various epicenters of Portland bohemian culture, the indie music is pumping through the speakers from a converted old-but-new record player, all the seats pointed towards the Probat coffee roaster which is already turning as it tumbles and roasts green coffee beans, I see traces and evidences of urban revitalization all around me. This city lives up to its hype of a vibrant central city, with its artisan economy, doable multi-modal transportation infrastructure, hipster populace, and a continuously growing trend of more people moving back into the heart of the city.

Portland is representative of numerous districts and neighborhoods within cities that are revitalizing. From Brooklyn on the east coast to SoMa in San Francisco on the west coast (and seemingly every city in between), there are seismic changes at hand that are reorienting, restructuring, and recalibrating cities. Not only that, but there has been an overall cultural shift in the values of Americans when it comes to where to live and how to get around. "For the first time in modern history, the number of people living in the city's downtown area grew faster than the population of its suburbs."[1] These changes are felt and experienced more acutely in certain places over others, but it's more than likely that your city is in the midst of this shift as well. In each city and district this phenomenon looks and feels different from the massive Inner Harbor revitalization project in Baltimore that has transformed the city, to the continued transformation of downtowns in cities such as Omaha or on a smaller scale like Mississippi Avenue in North Portland.

A life cycle of growth, stagnation, decline, and decay has been played out in numerous central cities, and in many cases we have now seen (or are seeing) new growth or revitalization in these same places. Brooklyn, which lost the Dodgers to Los Angeles in the late 1950s, now has an NBA franchise and a new stadium that are reflective of the reality that "Brooklyn is back." Kay Hymowitz notes that Brooklyn's transformation is the cumulative effect of numerous decisions, policy changes, and demographic shifts. In her article "How Brooklyn Got Its Groove Back" in the *City Journal* she writes:

> The third reason for Brooklyn's modern revival was the arrival of a new generation of gentrifiers, a large group of college-educated folks who, like the previous generation, found the urban, neighborly, and safer streets of the borough mightily attractive. The number of college-educated residents in Williamsburg increased by 80 percent between 2000 and 2008. Today, 30 percent of the residents of Park Slope, Cobble Hill, and Boerum Hill have master's degrees or higher.[2]

---

[1] Case Western Reserve University, "Moving to the City? Join the Crowd."

[2] Hymowitz, "How Brooklyn Got Its Groove Back," para, 20.

Sharon Zukin notes that this is a far cry from what Brooklyn used to be: "For most of the twentieth century Brooklyn had a sorry reputation as a place where artists and writers were born but were eager to escape from."[3]

The world we live in is influenced by what happens in cities. As Christians we dwell in cities around the world and wrestle with the implications of what it means to follow Christ in the city and plant churches. While there are numerous common denominators in place, there are also distinctive changes in cities that warrant a deeper look, exploration, analysis, and application for mission and church planting. For the most part, I will narrow the focus of my analysis to cities in North American contexts. As the title indicates and what I mentioned in the Introduction, throughout this book I will address specific issues, trends, and movements that are reshaping North American cities (as well as global cities). Since space is limited, this will not be an exhaustive list. However, these are topics of relevance to our cities (and admittedly of personal interest to me) that need further theological reflection in order to extract the missiological implications for today.

Cities are not what they were even thirty years ago. Cleveland, at the turn of the twentieth century was the fifth largest city in the US, one of the epicenters of the steel industry, and had positioned itself to be a major influencer

---

[3] Zukin, *Naked City*, 39.

nationally and globally.[4] It was a city with a bright future; seemingly the only place to go was up. It was a proud city. It was a city on the move. However, as the steel industry waned, many of the steel mills closed, tens of thousands left the city, whether to the suburbs or to other cities, and Cleveland was hollowed out, a vacant wasteland of sorts. The urban core was laid waste with aging substandard housing, under-performing schools,[5] and a bleak economic outlook. This once proud city had lost its pride and swagger and has endured a history of painful exoduses, whether it be the steel industry, the Browns leaving for Baltimore in 1995, or LeBron James taking his talents to Miami in 2010. *Washington Post* writer Michael Lee commented about the impact of just one player leaving an already vulnerable city: "James's decision to leave became the latest letdown for a city that knows despair, having experienced several major disappointments."[6] Luckily, LeBron came back and brought hope back with him, not only for the franchise, but also for the city.

The India Street neighborhood in Portland, Maine, is the oldest residential neighborhood[7] in the city that today sits

---

[4] "Great industrial cities not only grew larger; as their boundaries expanded, they also became more complex, with distinct areas for work and homes and different residential areas for workers, managers and professionals, and capitalists." Florida, *The Great Reset*, 20-21.

[5] Including the incident where the roof of one of the schools collapsed during the school day. CNN.com, "High school gym roof collapses in Cleveland."

[6] Lee, "LeBron James will leave Cleveland Cavaliers to join Dwyane Wade, Chris Bosh with the Miami Heat," para. 10.

[7] It got its start in the 17th Century and was called Broad Street. It was renamed India Street in 1837.

adjacent to the downtown and waterfront. The small neighborhood was a blue-collar African-American community prior to 1840. It later became a Jewish and Italian neighborhood. Construction of the Franklin Arterial cut the neighborhood off from the downtown and the Old Port. Like a flower that's been picked, eventually the neighborhood began to wither as it was no longer accessible to the nutrients of the city. It was and is a mixture of residential homes,[8] commercial buildings, and an industrial area. Many of the homes are in disrepair, substandard, and/or low-income housing even though there are some destination restaurants and other signs of hope cropping up such as higher density residential units now under construction. Hopes were running high a few years ago when a politician and her billionaire husband moved into the neighborhood and bought up a bunch of property. To the dismay of many residents, however, these properties sit undeveloped as the neighborhood continues to slide downward. A few pockets of growth and renewal are happening but only on a small scale. However, the neighborhood, thanks to numerous initiatives, is on the verge of a great comeback.

Both these cases are examples of neighborhoods or cities that have gone through numerous life stages; from vibrancy to decay, from decay to blight, and now from blight to ... hope? They are on the comeback, each in their own way. Cleveland has gained a lot of momentum through its Gateway District initiative in conjunction with the baseball stadium that was built in the 1990s. This is an example of a city utilizing a

---

[8] Greek Revival, Italianate, and Second Empire styles.

sports stadium as a catalyst for redevelopment and reinvestment. In this case, it proved to be one of the better initiatives. "Over 1,600 residents currently call the Gateway District home and take advantage of City living at an affordable price. Close to sports complexes, restaurants, downtown employment opportunities, theatre and nightlife, living in the Gateway District means you can walk to work or walk home after a night on the town. You're in the heart of Cleveland, so an authentic, urban living experience is yours to enjoy."[9]

> From 1990 to 2010, the downtown population practically doubled, growing from about 4,600 to more than 9,000. As developers and government agencies pour more than $5 billion into attractions, businesses and residences, young people are flocking to the city to become part of the increased activity. Looking for an affordable urban lifestyle, young people in their 20s and early 30s are on waiting lists for apartments. Old, empty offices are being converted to living space, and developers are having a hard time keeping up with demand.[10]

The India Street neighborhood in Portland, Maine, is poised to make significant leaps forward with mixed-use redevelopment underway and more to come. The neighborhood has become a pilot community of Sustain Southern Maine. "The India Street Neighborhood is a historically rich area of the Portland peninsula that has a

[9] Historic Gateway Neighborhood Corporation + Gateway District, "Live," para. 1.

[10] "Moving to the City? Join the Crowd."

surprising amount of space for development or redevelopment considering its proximity to downtown. We will be helping the City, the India Street Neighborhood organization and other interested parties develop a vision for the area that will embrace housing and job growth while respecting the area's history, scale, and its current vibe."[11] The neighborhood is on the verge of a more thorough and transformative renewal.

These are two examples of a multitude of neighborhoods, districts, and cities on an upswing across the country. Some have been building momentum for decades while others are gingerly leaving the starting blocks. But one thing is certain: there is a growing rediscovery of downtowns across the country whether in large cities such as the Financial District in Manhattan that is gaining more residential housing as it transitions from a nine-to-five district to a 24-7 district, to projects in small cities like Uptown in Normal, Illinois. As part of my work a couple of years ago on a sustainable cities project, we engaged with a cohort of cities across the country to help them implement sustainability plans which were centered around the theme of downtown revitalization. As a result I pored over quite a number of plans from these cities and others both large and small. The common denominator, whether making downtown Waco, Texas, more pedestrian-friendly through infill and densification, or green infrastructure plans in the SoBro neighborhood in Louisville, Kentucky, is that cities are involved in a new arms race of sorts to transform their cores. Which raises the question: What are the missiological implications of these changes?

---

[11] Sustain Southern Maine, "Portland: India Street neighborhood," para. 1.

We cannot broach the topic of urban revitalization without addressing the topic of equity. Behind the veneer of these renewal projects are oftentimes lower-income ethnic minorities becoming even more marginalized. Joel Kotkin, in an article entitled, "The Hollow Boom of Brooklyn: Behind the Veneer of Gentrification, Life Gets Worse for Many," writes about how, while the city is being held up as a bastion of coolness, there is also a pushed-aside reality behind the veneer. "So while artisanal cheese shops serve the hipsters and high-end shops thrive, one in four Brooklynites receives food stamps."[12] Richard Greenwald, professor of sociology and history at St. Joseph's College in New York, observes, "But, let's be honest, this discussion of Brooklyn (the Brooklyn of culture and arts, where novelists sit in cafes; the Brooklyn that Colson Whitehead wrote about in 2008) really is not the borough, but only a few neighborhoods: Williamsburg, Greenpoint, Bushwick, Bed-Sty and Fort Greene/Clinton Hill. These neighborhoods have gripped our imagination for almost 20 years, while the rest are absent from consciousness."[13]

How did we get to this point? How did Brooklyn, Wicker Park in Chicago, or Northeast Portland transition from what has been be described as "seedy, unsafe, war zones" of substandard housing, crime, and social unrest to now the epicenter of what would be deemed as successful urban revitalization? This is a far cry from where these neighborhoods were at even just a few years ago. In 1997

---

12 Kotkin, "The Hollow Boom of Brooklyn," para, 13.

13 Greenwald, "The Lifecycle of a 'Cool' Neighborhood," para, 9.

Harvard economist Michael Porter wrote, "The economic distress of America's inner-cities may be the most pressing issue facing the nation. The lack of business and jobs in disadvantaged urban areas fuels not only a crushing cycle of poverty but also crippling social problems, such as drug abuse and crime. And, as the inner cities continue to deteriorate, the debate on how to aid them grows increasingly divisive."[14] How did we transition from the downtowns as the economic and social hub of the city to urban decay and blight to revitalization and renewal?

By the end of the 19th Century downtowns were still *the* place. They were the central focus of cities culturally and economically. This was where one went for shopping, the theater, to buy a wedding dress, and so on. It also housed the bulk of the city's economic activity. It was a chaordic conglomeration of business and residential.[15] A lot of the heavy industry and warehouse districts sat adjacent to the downtowns or in close proximity. While post-WWII suburbanization, an expanding freeway system, and a growing shift towards an auto-centric lifestyle certainly began to diminish the role of the downtown, the out-migration began

---

[14] Porter, "The Competitive Advantages of the Inner City," 284.

[15] "Most city dwellers tended to live where they worked: craftsman and artisanal producers lived on top of or close to their shops, lawyers and doctors used their homes as offices. Pubs and cafes became neighborhood social centers or meeting places for subcommunities within large and diverse urban populations, a purpose they still serve today." *The Great Reset*, 21.

in earnest in the early 20th Century.[16] Michael Burayidi notes that, "Since the 1920s, there has been a steady decline in the economic health of downtowns in the United States. The middle class and businesses that once provided the thriving economic force of cities have moved to the surrounding suburban fringe, leaving in their wake, lower income households, vacant lots, and abandoned buildings."[17]

Burayidi goes on to explain the changing dynamics in American downtowns that caused them to hollow out and lose their revered status. Land in the city center was difficult and expensive to assemble for developers whereas suburban settings were wide open for development. And while downtowns were shaped by pedestrian activity and mass transit, the federal highway program and homeownership subsidies for the middle class accelerated suburbanization.[18] Not only did people move out of the city center, but so did businesses and economic activity. Initially there was little cause for concern as many assumed that suburbanites would simply drive back into the downtown,[19] but the decentralization of

---

16 "The traditional model used to describe downtowns is that of the monocentric city, which exhibited a hub-and-spoke streetcar system, centralized retail with commercial and industrial uses in the central business district (CBD) surrounded by compact residential areas. Since World War II, there has been a major shift in the composition of metropolitan areas to a polycentric form, with sprawling commercial strips and housing developments filling much of the space between cities and spawning new business districts." Faulk, "The Process and Practice of Downtown Revitalization," 630.

17 Burayidi, *Downtowns*, 1.

18 Ibid.

19 Fogelson, *Downtown*, 317-318.

economic activity from the downtown left in its wake a whole litany of economic and social ills.[20] As the middle class and businesses left the city those left behind tended to be poorer minorities.

These seismic shifts, like earthquakes ripping apart the urban landscape, began happening at an accelerating rate. All of these movements and transitions fed off of one another. As people moved out of the city in search of more space and better jobs, the people who were left in the central cities oftentimes were the ones who were not able to be as mobile. As a result, as Burayidi noted above, those left in the central cities tended to be lower-income ethnic minorities. Not only that, but the old urban fabric was deteriorating as buildings were falling apart due to age and neglect. This made the middle class move out with more rapidity. What was left behind were lower income minorities in deteriorating central cities. These transitions were coupled with a loss of tax revenues, so that the cost of amenities far exceeded what was

---

[20] "During the late 1930s and early 1940s, however, many Americans began to have second thoughts about residential dispersal. In their efforts to account for the sorry state of the central business district, they were struck by two unexpected (and extremely ominous) developments. One was that a large and growing number of people who had moved to the periphery were no longer going downtown – or were going downtown less often. Instead they were patronizing the outlying business districts, shopping at chain stores, doing business at branch banks, and relaxing at neighborhood restaurants and movie theaters. The other development was that the movement outward was highly selective. The upper and middle classes were moving to the periphery and the suburbs. But the lower class, many of whose members belonged to one or another of the nation's ethnic and racial minorities, were staying put – some because they did not want to move, others because they could not afford to. More often that not, these people lived within a long walk or short ride of the central business district. But they had little money to spend in the downtown stores and specialty shops, little reason to retain downtown lawyers and accountants, and little cause to deal with downtown banks and insurance companies." Ibid., 318.

generated through taxes.[21] The result was a large segment of low-income minorities living in deteriorating central cities with limited access to jobs, good schools and the necessary amenities. This created the conditions for social unrest which further solidified the dichotomy that cities were "bad" and suburbs were "good."

Alexander von Hoffman in his book *House by House, Block by Block: The Rebirth of America's Urban Neighborhoods* follows the storyline of the South Bronx. What was once a growing vibrant city of immigrants in the early 20th century had fallen so precipitously that by the 70s, "The South Bronx went on to become first the national, then an international icon of America's worst slum."[22] Many local residents felt powerless to reverse the changes sweeping over the neighborhood and ripping it apart. Even emergency services such as police and fire had been cut off. It was anarchy and chaos.

David Harvey in his article "The Right to the City" writes:

> The right to the city is not merely a right of access to what already exists, but a right to change it after our heart's desire. We need to be sure we can live with our own creations (a problem for every planner, architect and utopian thinker). But the right to remake ourselves by creating a qualitatively different kind of urban sociality is one of the most precious of all human rights. The sheer pace and chaotic forms of urbanization throughout the world have made it hard to reflect on the nature of this task. We have been made and re-made without knowing exactly why, how, wherefore and to what end. How then, can we better exercise this right to the city?[23]

---

[21] *Downtowns*, 2.

[22] von Hoffman, *House by House, Block by Block*, 19.

[23] Harvey, "The Right to the City," 939.

The city has always been a contested space and has never been free of "confusions, conflicts, violence."[24] For many in the inner city this was an everyday reality. In Harvey's words, they didn't have the "right to the city" in terms of equal and equitable access. Various programs to remedy living conditions only exasperated the plight of the poor. "Intolerable housing conditions in old and very old buildings in the growing cities, coupled with the wish to make 'better use' of central urban land and drive the poor out of sight, gave birth to the idea of slum clearance."[25] Too often what replaced the housing of the poor did not benefit them. Instead, many were displaced to make way for amenities catering to the middle class. "The slum areas were frequently replaced by shopping centers, office buildings, and cultural and entertainment centers, all of which were in high demand in the booming years that followed World War II."[26]

It was when these inner city neighborhoods and districts hit rock bottom that things began slowly to turn around. Various attempt were made, and continue to be made, to remedy these ailing and blighted areas ranging from massive slum clearance programs to urban revitalization initiatives, and from public / private partnerships to small-scale private investment building by building and block by block. This is also coupled with the process of gentrification that I will cover in a later chapter.

---

[24] Ibid.

[25] Carmon, "Three generations of urban renewal policies," 145-146.

[26] Ibid., 146.

What changed was our perception of the city. Was it the realization that sprawling low-density auto-centric suburbs were not as livable as we initially thought? Maybe there was something in those old buildings in the central cities that still housed appeal and an identity that we did not want to be divorced from. Jane Jacobs was certainly prophetic in this regard. "Williamsburg's growing prominence as a hipster locale during the 1990s confirms Jane Jacob's idea that old buildings with low rents will act as incubators of new activities."[27]

It is interesting to see how cities are tackling the process of renewing their downtowns and central cities. Some cities are well ahead of the curve while others are just entering into the fray after decades of clearing old buildings only to replace them with super-block projects that are not pedestrian-friendly. The reality is that decades of neglect have rendered many of these districts and neighborhoods blighted. "As Jerrold Loebl, a Chicago architect and developer, pointed out in the mid 1940s, conditions in the central city were pretty bad. And nowhere in the central city were they worse than in old residential neighborhoods surrounding the central business district. Here were the slums and 'blighted areas.'"[28]

To jumpstart many of these projects means that areas would have to be deemed "blighted" (eminent domain) in order to relocate residents, raze the properties, and start anew. In the hands of the right people this can be a helpful process, but in the hands of the greedy it became a way to make money

---

[27] *Naked City*, 38.

[28] Downtown, 319.

at the expense of those who were forced to vacate. It all hinged
on how one defined "blight."

> The definition remained imprecise and ambiguous because
> most viewed "blight" not as synonymous with "slum" but
> as a set conditions, often analogized as a disease or a
> cancer, that resulted in slums: A blighted area was "on the
> down grade, which has not reached the slum stage" or "a
> potential slum" or "an insidious malady that attacks urban
> residential districts ... first as a barely noticeable
> deterioration and then progresses gradually through many
> stages toward a final condition known as the slum."[29]

Once the "blight" label was applied it became a green light for
redevelopment, but it was not without controversy or mixed
motives.[30]

As city after city, particularly in the Northeast and
Midwest, begin to shed their "industrial city" moniker as our
economy continues to move towards Post-Fordism[31] or a
creative economy, many of these cities continue to rebuild and
renew their urban landscape. Many sites connected to steel or

---

[29] Gordon, *Mapping Decline*, 190.

[30] "What makes such local discretion all the more troubling is the fact that the
designation of blight often occurred on a proposal-by-proposal basis, at the
behest of developers. Blighting, in other words, was driven not by objective
urban conditions but by the prospect of private investment. In practice, this
meant that investment was actually steered away from the most dismal urban
conditions as private interests sought the 'blight that's right' – an area with at
least some of the conditions needed to make a plausible cause for subsidized
redevelopment, but not so run-down as to put private investment at risk."
Ibid., 197.

[31] "Fordist affluence was increasingly manifest in suburban homeownership,
not the inner-city neighborhood." Lloyd, *Neo-Bohemia*, 41.

heavy industry closed down and for decades these old plants and mills stood vacant sort of like the fossils of an extinct dinosaur.

But it was precisely this economic change which was and is one of the sparks of urban revitalization. These economic shifts mean more and more of our economy is being geared towards the creative, knowledge-based, or artisan economy which I will cover in more detail in a later chapter. What is noteworthy here is that cities, in efforts to revitalize their downtowns and city centers, are specifically, strategically, and unabashedly throwing their lot in with the creative class. Whether Wichita, Waco, Louisville, or Portland (Maine), their revitalization plans are predicated on wooing this socio-economic grouping—variously described as the creative class, hipsters, yupsters, and bohemians—into their city centers.

Richard Lloyd, in his book *Neo-Bohemia*, writes, "the role of cities as generative milieus for innovations of all sorts is crucial to understanding the reemergence of spaces that appeared to have outlived their usefulness in the wake of deindustrialization and the expansion of telematics and digital communication technologies, from the high-priced skyscrapers of the downtown to a gritty neo-bohemian neighborhood like Wicker Park."[32]

While I have purposely leap-frogged large segments of history and a great body of literature, what is apparent is that downtown revitalization is accelerating. There are a myriad of reasons why, and I am only briefly touching on a couple of them, such as the economic changes wrought on by

---

[32] Ibid., 44.

deindustrialization, a movement towards a creative economy, and how this growing creative class workforce is helping to reshape cities. Not only that, but cities are reshaping themselves to attract this group of people who are mobile, white-collar, and have discretionary income. "Over the last three decades schemes to attract the wealthy middle classes back to the inner city have become central to urban redevelopment strategies."[33]

These strategies are more than simply wooing this middle class back into the city, but also capitalize on their consumption, lifestyle, and spending habits. "Urban revitalization strategies are aimed not just at attracting middle-class gentrifiers as resident taxpayers, but also at bringing them back to urban areas as consuming, and in that spending, visitors."[34] This offers some insight into the catalytic nature of how this class is transforming cities, or how cities are transforming themselves to attract and retain hipsters, yupsters, and bohemians. This ranges from creating entertainment zones or districts, new stadiums and surrounding developments, cultural amenities such as museums and art galleries, and new housing. "Cities compete by making themselves distinctive places of consumption in which to satisfy new upscale demands for commercialized leisure, recreation and other experiences."[35]

---

[33] Lees, "The Ambivalence of Diversity and the Politics of Urban Renaissance," 613.

[34] Ibid., 614.

[35] Ibid.

Portland, Oregon, is seen as the poster-child of urban revitalization with our robust artisan economy, hipster and bohemian neighborhoods and districts, foodie culture, and a transportation infrastructure that includes bicycles, light rail, and streetcar. I have lost track of how many downtown revitalization plans for other cities I have looked at that included pictures and scenes from Portland whether snapshots of our streetcars, redeveloped Pearl District, or bicycle lanes. It would appear that many cities are attempting to emulate Portland.

The ways in which cities are attempting to revitalize their city centers are manifold. Some cities create large entertainment districts while at other times there are ad hoc entertainment zones that develop more organically.

Sports stadiums are used as "a catalyst for the *physical redevelopment* of portions of the city's core."[36] Another method to catalyze urban redevelopment is the use of major events. "Cities often use the opportunity of staging events to undertake large-scale regeneration projects."[37] City after city across the continent have deployed some variation of this despite the data that shows their actual economic benefits are dubious. It is argued that the creative class, those who the city is most trying to woo, are quasi-resistant to such forms of entertainment and recreation.

---

[36] Chapin, "Sports Facilities as Urban Redevelopment Catalysts," 194.

[37] Smith, *Events and Urban Regeneration*, 16.

Emphasis on big-ticket items like athletic stadiums locates the production of new urban space solely in the hands of developers and political elites. It obscures more evolutionary process of cultural development, including the expanding role played by traditional patterns of urban subcultural affiliation and artistic innovation in the postindustrial economy—both in terms of local consumption offerings and the concentration of cultural and design enterprises.[38]

What immediately comes to the surface are issues of equity. Before we completely dismiss these efforts, programs, and initiatives as running roughshod over lower income families in degraded urban neighborhoods, we also need to consider the implications of revitalization. Because many of the middle class had previously vacated city centers along with businesses there was a drastic loss in tax revenue. A shrinking business sector, empty offices, and depreciating home values means less money for city services. This impacts schools as well. This in turn creates an avalanche effect that as neighborhoods continue to decline those who can move out do so which results in even less capital flowing through the neighborhood. The neighborhood continues to spiral downward. Conversely, when more people move back into urban neighborhoods housing values rise, new businesses start, and there is a sense of a "stabilizing affect" as more capital flows back in.

Today the tables have turned in many city centers across the country. There is this in-migration as the appeal for an "authentic" urban life woos many back to the city. In a recent

---

[38] Lloyd, "Neo-Bohemia," 217.

ast on *The Urbanist*,[39] Sharon Zukin was being interviewed and the discussion centered around the term "authentic." As she writes in her book *Naked City: The Death and Life of Authentic Urban Places* and as she explains in the interview, "authenticity" is a very subjective term that has been co-opted by developers to creatively market retrofits in older urban neighborhoods.

Gritty is in vogue. As cities continue to morph and move away from being manufacturing-centered the city that is emerging in its place is more about consumption than production. Indeed production still is prevalent, and in many ways just as imbedded into the fabric of the city as before, but it is more knowledge- or creative-based, from tech start-up companies to design and fashion to publishing and so forth.

To talk about urban revitalization is a large umbrella that encompasses much. It goes beyond creating or recreating the built environment of the city; it encompasses housing, race relations, economics, real estate, community development, justice and equity, architecture, education, politics, and so much more.

The changing city of the 21st-century is more about cultural consumption. "Authenticity" is highly valued. This is one of the arguments made to explain the allure of gentrification. To live in a mixed-use old urban neighborhood that is still racially and socio-economically diverse is for many a desirable reality. Their desire is not to see the neighborhood change because it was these dynamics which drew them there to begin with. This is also why advocates like Jane Jacobs

---

[39] Episode 78.

fought development because she saw the value of these "authentic" urban neighborhoods.

Today this search and need for authenticity comes in numerous forms. Another recent episode of *The Urbanist*,[40] which focused on the topic of sex and the city, featured a segment on Amsterdam's red light district. In the interview several tech and fashion entrepreneurs explained why they chose to relocate or start their businesses among prostitutes walking the streets day and night. Their presence coupled with an abundance of adult shops certainly gave this district an "authentic" and "gritty" sense about it. These features were precisely the allure these business owners were looking for. It is part of the search for authenticity in the city.

Urban revitalization in many ways capitalizes on this appeal for authenticity by creating what Sharon Zukin alludes to as a *faux authenticity* in *Naked City*.

I have a front-row seat to the transformative effects taking place in my own neighborhood in Portland. The Hollywood District has gone through significant changes in the short time frame we have lived here. Two new apartment buildings feature studio and one-bedroom units with no parking spaces. The owners apparently assume they'll attract 20-somethings who get around via bicycle, mass transit, or car-sharing. The neighborhood still retains a quirky grittiness to it and a certain level of "authenticity" with rundown bars and billiard halls, an abundance of panhandlers, and architecture that is bland and uninspiring. But all around are signs of change from new

---

[40] Episode 74.

businesses that cater to the younger generation including bike shops, coffee shops, hip pizza places, and fashion stores.

These are the cities that we dwell in. The follow-up question is ... how do we respond? What is the role of Christians individually and the church, whether locally or collectively across the city in urban revitalization? How do these changes impact and influence church planting in the city? Responses vary greatly.

A quick perusal of social media reveals all of the ways, roles, or capacity that people I know are engaged in or involved in responding whether they realize it or not. Many church planters I know are moving into revitalizing urban neighborhoods across the country to start churches. That is not merely a Portland phenomenon even though we have a growing cluster of new churches in the city center, but it is happening in your city as well ... Williamsburg in Brooklyn, SoMa in San Francisco, Belltown or Capital Hill in Seattle, LoDo in Denver, Kitsilano in Vancouver, and so forth. Churches like these cater to and appeal to the creative class. They are certainly categorized as being hip, trendy, hipster, techy, and the like. These kinds of churches are needed as they are reflective of the changing dynamics of these neighborhoods.

Other friends on social media are responding in a completely different manner. They are purposely moving into still depressed urban or inner-ring suburban neighborhoods. Oftentimes these are the catch basins for the migrating urban poor who are no longer in the central city. Or these are central city neighborhoods that have still yet to revitalize. Many of these sprawling older inner-ring suburbs are lower density, full of ugly strip malls and convenience stores, and generally unappealing. I see Christians and churches there embodying a more incarnational presence with the neighborhood, seeking its *shalom*, and being more organic in their liturgical expression. They are intentionally identifying with the poor and marginalized. These kinds of churches are needed because they reflect the dynamics of their neighborhoods.

What then are the missiological implications for urban revitalization? As cities change and continue to reinvent themselves, what role should the church play in the process? Do we identify with those on lower income and the marginalized? Do we identify with the growing creative class that cities are recalibrating themselves for? How does a church planter answer those questions? The changes taking place in our cities, whether in North America or globally, are simply the latest aberrations of the evolving nature of cities. What that means is that with each change we are thrust into a new environment which we must seek to understand and interpret within a theological framework. That theological framework then informs us how we are to respond. Urban revitalization must be held up and critiqued through this framework. When we do so we recognize that God cares for the flourishing of cities.

Those who have lived through such inexplicable events as the burning of the South Bronx, the Watts riot in Los Angeles, or watched the river burning in Cleveland, do not look with nostalgia upon decaying urban neighborhoods. Physical and economic revitalization in and of itself is a preferred future for many, but the side effects (e.g. displacement, loss of identity) are what creates the most controversy. Theologically, does God favor urban revitalization? If we hold to the notion that God is the author of cities who set forth healthy blueprints for their functionality, and since Genesis 1:28 is about human flourishing, then we can contend that certain aspect of urban revitalization is healthy and God-pleasing.

Sitting adjacent to the campus of Portland State University is the mostly unknown South Auditorium Urban Renewal Area. Once a robust Italian community on the south side of what currently is downtown Portland, it was razed and redeveloped as Portland's first urban renewal project: "1,573 residents of South Portland, including 336 families and 289 businesses were pushed out, and 445 buildings were demolished."[41] Today, the only reminder of this former working class ethnic neighborhood is The Church of St. Michael the Archangel (1894) and St. Mary's Academy (1859) which served this Catholic community. These buildings are surrounded by newer modern buildings and are all that remain of area that had been deemed "blighted."

This one example thrusts to the forefront equity issues surrounding urban revitalization. In most cases it involved historically entrenched ethnic groups (both white and black) and their displacement. Not only that, but in using eminent domain, these usually poor neighborhoods were labeled as "blighted" which gave the government the authority to forcibly remove its residents, raze their homes and businesses, and build anew. Most often the hipster enclaves that are so beloved

---

[41] Tackett, "South Auditorium Urban Renewal," para., 1.

today with their creative class, renovated homes, and the like, are the products of a dubious past.

One of the topics that the discussion on human flourishing addresses is the nature of a civil society. If God is about human flourishing, which includes such things as culture and cities, how should we define it? Is there even a one-size-fits-all template for a civil society? Also, who gets to define what a civil society even is? That is a point of contention when it comes to such topics as foreign aid to poverty-stricken places like Lagos, Nigeria. What Western or Northern ethnic whites may deem as a civil society may be completely devoid of local expressions of life and human flourishing. Simply because not everyone is running around with iPhones or watching reality shows on 42-inch flat panel televisions does not mean they are any less "civil" than we are.

Who gets to determine when an area is blighted and in need of renewal? A quick perusal of urban revitalization projects in the US reveals that there was much money to be made. Frequently this was at the expense of the poor who were "in the way" of development. City after city across the country and world we find this same phenomenon taking place whether in Brooklyn, Mumbai, or Beijing.

My intent is not to offer a long discourse on the nuances of a civil society, eminent domain, blight, and the economics of urban revitalization, but to simply point out that there are multiple actors and components involved in the process. It is not as clear-cut as an empty dilapidated urban neighborhood, devoid of people, being bulldozed, and in its place new housing or businesses going in. Each space and place in the city is contested, each with their own ethnic, economic, political, environmental, and spiritual undertones and overtones.

A common theme throughout Scripture is God's preferential treatment of the poor. How do we reconcile this with urban revitalization? Are they mutually compatible? Are there such things as urban renewal projects that create space for the poor? The Pearl district in Portland has been an attempt to rectify this by setting aside 30 to 40 percent of the new housing in this swank district for affordable housing.

The point is that urban revitalization is at the forefront of many cities' attempts to renew and revitalize struggling urban neighborhoods. On the surface this can be healthy and helpful to cities seeking to remake and reinvent themselves in a bid to boost their overall economic outlook. But there are also downsides in that these same projects usually tend to cater to the white-collar creative class which can make these new zones homogeneous and exclusionary.

How is the church to respond? For those of you who are planting in the heart of the city or in the process of moving there ... what will you do? How does this chapter help you better understand your city, how to exegete your neighborhood, and in turn plant a life-giving Gospel-focused church that seeks the transformation of urban people and places?

Chapter 3

Suburbanization and Human Flourishing

Suburbia has cultivated the reputation of being scorned by both urbanites and rural dwellers alike. It is like the purgatory of cities ... close, but not quite. Discourse on the topic continues to swirl making this geographic setting and cultural phenomenon an easy target for both verbal and written jabs. Rarely it seems does suburbia jab back. But is it really that awful a place?

For roughly ten years I lived in suburbia where rampant auto-based sprawl defined the spatial layout of cities in the Southwest like Phoenix and Tucson. Growing up in small-town Iowa I did not harbor any pent-up frustration over the malaise of suburbia; it just made sense to me. It was in many ways an easier life as housing was newer and inexpensive, the schools were good, there was ample elbow room, and I was only minutes from epic mountain biking terrain which I could access by pedaling out of my garage.

Tama, Iowa, where I grew up, in many ways resembled suburbia in that housing and population distribution were low-density and spread out as most lived in single-family detached homes. As a result, it was and is quite normative upon turning sixteen to be swept into the mobility of the car culture. No grand conspiracy theories, it was how most of us lived.

Suburban life was not that much different except it was newer, nicer, had more amenities, and easy access to urban culture and entertainment without living in the city. For many, it was the best of both worlds. For those with small-town or rural leanings and preferences, but yet had to live in cities because that's where the jobs were, the suburbs became a doable "in-between" setting, a smaller-town feel but with access to the larger city. However, my sons, who have been shaped and influenced by an urban lifestyle see the urban vs. suburban dichotomy more succinctly than I did.

My sons see the world through an urban lens. Urban is preferred over the suburban. The only time they ever want to head out to the suburbs is because that's where some of their favorite skateboarding spots are located. Other than that, life for them revolves around how far they can go on skateboards whether to school, friends' houses, downtown, or the skate shop. That and light rail (or buses) are their preferred modes of transportation and which they and many of their friends are accustomed to riding alone.

Suburbia is a much maligned space within our cities. It is a controversial aberration in the development of cities with its lower densities and mass-produced housing at the expense of agricultural lands and wilderness, and a predominantly auto-based lifestyle. Simultaneous with its explosive growth came new churches ... but churches have always been started on the growth edge of cities. Recently on a bicycle ride around inner NE and North Portland I stopped to read the cornerstones of two historic black churches. One cornerstone was written in a language I didn't understand and the other was in German. At one point in the city's past, these had been ethnic European immigrant neighborhoods on Portland's "suburban" fringe even though today they sit on the outskirts of Portland's downtown. Started in the late 1800s these communities remind us that suburbanization has been around for quite a while.

Contrary to popular notions, suburbanization is a process that pre-dates the automobile. Cities have been continuously expanding outwards as populations swelled. Some of the classic, notable, and contentious urban spaces in American cities today were once the result of sprawl. But unlike back then, sprawl or suburbanization now carries with it a negative image of cultural and architectural sterility, homogeneity, boredom, anti-urban bias, auto-dominated lives, and mass consumption.

Are the origins and development of suburbia truly seedy and questionable or are they the result of peoples' preferences for more space accelerated by changing transportation technologies? This chapter explores the origins, trajectory, and future of suburbanization.

Jeff Speck in his book *Walkable City* writes, "the way we move largely determines the way we live."[1] This observation is a fitting way a conversation on how transportation impacted the evolution of suburbia, since how people get around forms the backbone of its development. The common perception of suburbia in contemporary American culture is that of sprawl,

---

[1] Speck, *Walkable City*, 55.

mass cultural consumption, and lifestyles revolving around the automobile. "Transportation technologies shape our communities, and modern sprawl is the child of the automobile."[2] However, the beginnings of the suburbanization process go back long before the advent of the car.

Glaeser contends that sprawl began centuries ago when people began using other modes of transportation which allowed them to travel greater distances. That in turn impacted the urban fabric of cities.[3] William Flanagan echoes that argument when he writes, "Changes in transportation technology transformed the shape of cities and their patterns of use."[4] Each change in transportation technology allowed for people to live farther and farther away from the city center. The horse-drawn omnibus was introduced in Paris in 1819 and in New York City in the 1920s.[5] Over the next few decades omnibuses began operating in other cities like Boston, Philadelphia, Baltimore, St. Louis, Cincinnati, and San Francisco.[6]

Prior to these omnibuses these cities were walking cities. The fact that the vast majority of urban dwellers, apart from the elite, got around on foot had a direct impact on the spatial layouts of cities. Housing was close to places of work or

---

[2] Glaeser, *Triumph of the City*, 167.

[3] Ibid.

[4] Flanagan, *Urban Sociology*, 208.

[5] *Triumph of the City*, 169.

[6] *Urban Sociology*, 208.

transportation nodes such as docks.[7] For a destination to be "walkable" meant that it was within an hour's walk. As a result, cities tended to be crowded and living conditions for many, especially the poor, were compact and substandard. "Cities remained unhealthy places throughout the century, becoming more so with time, especially for the poor. Death rates were higher in the city and life expectancies shorter than for rural populations."[8] The advent of the omnibuses meant that the populace could "spread out" from the crowded and congested city center. The omnibuses gave way to horse-drawn streetcars and then to the electric streetcar. "The net effect of these improvements was to allow residents who could afford it the chance to move yet farther from the business district."[9] These were some of America's first "suburbanites."

Because of these changing transportation technologies "sprawl" began to occur. Edward Glaeser comments that, "In the 1950s, when Jane Jacobs fought against running a road through Washington Square Park, she was fighting to save nineteenth-century sprawl from twentieth-century sprawl."[10] Flanagan notes that this sprawl at the turn of the twentieth century "retained a certain discipline reminiscent of the old walking city" and spread out in "narrow fingers or spokes of settlement."[11]

---

[7] Ibid., 207.

[8] Ibid.

[9] Ibid., 208.

[10] *Triumph of the City*, 170.

[11] *Urban Sociology*, 209.

The Hollywood District in Portland, where I currently live, is reflective of how these evolving transportation technologies allowed for early suburbanization. The neighborhood is anchored by the Hollywood Theater which was built in the 1920s as a direct result of a growing population on the east side of the Willamette River in the first part of the twentieth century. "At the start of this era the Hollywood District contained only a few homes and dirt roads. In 1906 a streetcar line ran the length of Sandy Boulevard. Called the Rose City Line, the streetcar allowed residential growth."[12] This "suburb" sits only two to three miles from Portland's downtown (ten minutes by bike) and does not symbolize what we typically think of as a suburb. Today, most view Hollywood as an inner-city Portland neighborhood.

Beginning in the twentieth century the population outside the city center was growing more rapidly than within it. "During the 1920s, there was already substantial suburban development around several large cities, such as Atlanta, Cleveland, Milwaukee, and Buffalo."[13] At the same time there were signs of a coming major future urban population shift in cities on both the east and west coasts.[14]

Thus far the main common denominator throughout has been that changing transportation technologies allowed for and created the opportunities for suburbanization. The

---

[12] Portland State University Senior Capstone, "Historical Highlights of Hollywood"

[13] *Urban Sociology*, 210.

[14] Ibid., 211.

twentieth century would herald a giant leap forward in additional transportation technologies that would propel the population ever-outward like a giant centrifuge. "While the nineteenth century saw several transit innovations, the twentieth-century city was dominated by one: the internal combustion engine."[15] By this time suburbanization was already entrenched in the growth patterns of cities. What began in the late 1800s and early 1900s would pale in comparison to the changes in sprawl wrought by the personal automobile.

In his book *Making Transit Fun*, Darrin Nordahl writes that the way to get people out of their cars is to make public transit fun. "Throughout the world, imaginative transit campaigns, accessories, and circulators are being devised to woo the entrenched motorist. The common denominator in each of these strategies is a single, positive emotion: joy. Joy helps transit compete against the allure of the automobile."[16] However, in the first part of the twentieth century this was quite the opposite. Transit was not fun. Crowded streetcars and subways were unsavory, smelly, and polluted. Peoples' movements were restricted to where existing transit lines could take them. The personal automobile changed everything. "In the ten years from 1905 to 1915, the number of registered automobiles [nationally] increased from 8,000 to 2.3 million. By 1925 there were 17.5 million; by 1930, 23 million."[17] This

---

[15] *Triumph of the City*, 172.

[16] Nordahl, *Making Transit Fun*, loc. 49.

[17] *Urban Sociology*, 213.

began to change significantly the patterns of how cities grew, developed, and expanded.

The growing popularity of the automobile meant that the roadway infrastructure also had to be revamped, improved, and expanded. This allowed for greater flexibility for hauling freight by trucks which meant firms dependent on trucking relocated out of the central city and helped further advance the decentralization of industry. Cars meant that people could travel farther within cities between home and work. "As the margins of city after city sprawled outward, the people, economic interests, and government bodies of the United States were making some important decisions about the future of transportation and the shape that cities would take."[18] By the early 1920s streetcar ridership had peaked and would never recover.

Fordism hit its high-water mark after World War II, as mass production also began to have a cultural effect. Uniformity and standardization were not only the hallmark of Henry Ford's assembly lines, but they soon would spill over into other areas ... like housing. There had already been an economic shift underway from Fordism to Post-Fordism, but the war allowed Fordism to tarry a little longer as many countries and their economies had been decimated from the war.

> Although the population was being transformed during the 1950s from a predominantly blue-collar to a white-collar workforce, and U.S. Americans were increasingly encouraged to think of themselves as middle- rather than

---

[18] Ibid., 214.

working-class, the new prosperity was modest. If they were to buy suburban housing in large numbers, it wouldn't be the expensive, prewar variety that had been limited largely to the upper middle class. In every large city, however, a number of builders found innovative ways to lower construction costs in order to capture a share of the new market. None competed more successfully than Abraham Levitt and Sons.[19]

Levitt was determined to become the Henry Ford of housing by streamlining the creation of large numbers of homes cheaply and efficiently.[20]

Already there was a backlash towards new suburban communities. E. Barbara Phillips notes that, "It is significant that the negative suburban image was the work of a small segment of people in the United States: urbane, upper-class, white intellectuals. Overwhelmingly, the critics were well-educated white, Angle-Saxon, Protestant (WASP) males who lived in either the rural countryside or the major metropolitan centers, not in the suburbs."[21] Regardless of what the critics said or felt, Americans were voting with their feet and moving en masse to the suburbs.

Thus far I have explored some of the backstory of suburbanization, mostly as it pertains to the changes in transportation technologies. Sprawl or suburbanization are not always one and the same, but are most often lumped together, fostering a source of much contention within academia and in

---

[19] Ibid., 221.

[20] *Triumph of the City*, 174.

[21] Phillips, *City Lights*, 220.

popular culture. As Richard T. LeGates and Frederic Stout say, "No spatial policy issue has preoccupied urbanists more than urban sprawl."[22] This raises questions that have been asked repeatedly since cities continued urbanizing over the past hundred-plus years: why do we have sprawl or suburbanization? Is it good? Is it bad?

Robert Bruegmann attacks some of the criticisms aimed at sprawl and suburbanization, arguing that the following factors were responsible: a frontier ethic embedded in the American psyche, an anti-urban bias, racism, greedy individuals and developers, bad government policies, and so forth.[23] In pragmatic fashion, he contends that suburbanites are truly not anti-urban.

> Most Americans do not like the dirt and disorder that characterized historic nineteenth-century industrial cities, and they may be indifferent if not hostile to the clubby culture of the downtown elite cultural groups, but there is little evidence that suburbanites are opposed to urbanity. They only want to rearrange the physical elements to make life more convenient and pleasant for themselves and to avoid the things that made nineteenth-century industrial cities so unpleasant for people who did not have a great deal of money.[24]

This forms the foundation for his argument in "The Cause of Sprawl" where he refutes the claim that it was caused by

---

22 LeGates and Stout, *The City Reader*, 211.

23 Bruegmann, "The Cause of Sprawl," 212.

24 Ibid., 213.

economic factors and the capitalistic system, the government, and transportation technologies. Instead, he contends that sprawl and suburbanization happened simply because people wanted it to happen and that political democratization was the vehicle to allow it to happen.

> Although sprawl has developed differently at different times and in different places, the history of sprawl suggests that the two factors that seem to track most closely with sprawl have been increasing affluence and political democratization. In places where citizens have become more affluent and have enjoyed basic economic and political rights, more people have been able to gain for themselves the benefits once reserved for wealthier citizens. I believe that the most important of these can be defined as privacy, mobility, and choice.[25]

Beginning with Abraham Levitt's Levittown the suburbanization process became, like Henry Ford's assembly lines, streamlined and efficient. This kept the costs lower and therefore within reach of many Americans. There were to be two more significant events (among many) that would be decisive factors in the growth and expansion of suburbia: favorable mortgage loans and the expanding freeways including the interstate freeway system. These two factors exponentially impacted the growth of the suburbs and the decline of the central city. "In 1944, Veterans Administration mortgage loans had been added to the other loans available through the Federal Housing Administration, and, together, these government guarantees helped to fuel an unprecedented

---

[25] Ibid., 220.

growth in the housing industry."[26] The resultant impact was that millions flocked to the suburbs to buy a slice of the American Pie. While the favorable loans, new suburban growth, and the freeway system were intended to improve the living conditions for millions of Americans, the same cannot be said for the central city. "Neither the federal housing policies nor interstate highway spending were designed to be antiurban, but they hurt cities."[27]

This furthered the trajectory of American cities in which life revolved around the car. Not only did people move out of the city center and into the suburbs, jobs went with them. "Although considered prosperous in the earlier part of the twentieth century, many urban commercial areas in the United States began a spiral of economic and physical decline in the 1950s as manufacturing jobs and middle-class families moved to the suburbs."[28] About half the jobs in the largest cities now lie more than ten miles away from the city center.[29] This seemingly benign reality of people and jobs increasingly being located in the suburbs has created a whole litany of contentions and challenges. As noted above, Bruegmann asserts that the impetus behind sprawl and suburbanization is simply that it is the preferred lifestyle and future of

---

[26] *Urban Sociology*, 219.

[27] *Triumph of the City*, 176.

[28] Hoyt, "Do Business Improvement District Organizations Make a Difference?" 185.

[29] *Triumph of the City*, 177.

Americans. Edward Glaeser refutes that; he writes, "Cars, not culture, are the root of sprawl."[30]

Regardless of who is right, and probably both are to some extent, the reality of cities across North America is that we are saddled with auto-oriented suburbs. Even in a progressive and innovative city like Portland, only 25 percent of our metro's population even lives within the borders of Portland proper. In other words, only 593,000 out of 2.2 million people live in Portland; the rest live in its suburbs. Even other world-class North American cites that are known for density and walkable urbanism are still plagued with suburban sprawl. "Canada currently has three of the world's ten urban areas with the most extensive sprawl—Calgary, Vancouver and Toronto."[31]

Since this is the current reality for the majority of North America's urban dwellers, what does it mean? Numerous problematic issues have surfaced in regards to living conditions in suburbia. Despite their alleged ethnic and socio-economic homogeneity, the suburbs are truly places of diversity and even inequity, while offering hope and a landing place for new immigrants. In a recent *New York Times* article entitled "Suburban Disequilibrium," Becky M. Nicolaides and Andrew Wiese write that, "iconic middle-income suburbs are shrinking in numbers and prospects. Today's suburbs provide a map not just to the different worlds of the rich and poor, which have always been with us, but to the increase in inequality between

---

[30] Ibid., 178.

[31] UN-HABITAT, *Planning Sustainable Cities*, 28.

economic and social classes."[32] Focusing on two adjacent suburbs in Los Angeles, one extremely wealthy and elitist and the other low-income, these authors contend that policies need to address these social inequalities. This hardly sounds like the perception that all suburbs are all-white homogeneous places like Levittown.

Historically the city centers served as the catch basins for incoming immigrants, especially those who were working class and low income. But that is changing. In his book *The Great Inversion and the Future of the American City*, Alan Ehrenhalt, observing the Atlanta metro area, explains that according to the 2010 Census Bureau figures, "of all foreign-born newcomers to the Atlanta area, only a small percentage were settling in the city. The rest were becoming suburbanites."[33] Harry Hiller, writing about Canadian cities, notes the same trend: "Many new immigrants move directly to the suburbs, where jobs and housing are more readily available."[34] We have seen this trend here in Portland as the central city becomes whiter. This is also reflective of the rising cost of living in the once-hollowed-out central city in comparison to the suburbs.

Good insight

> As we have now seen, inner-city neighborhoods such as Sheffield in Chicago and lower Manhattan in New York are becoming attractive to the affluent, and considerably more expensive that most of the metropolitan periphery. In most successful large cities, it is simply no financial bargain for newcomers to live downtown anymore. Most of the jobs they seek are in the suburbs anyway. At this

---

32 Nicolaides and Wiese, "Suburban Disequilibrium," para, 2–3.

33 Ehrenhalt, *The Great Inversion and the Future of the American City*, loc 1441.

34 Hiller, *Urban Canada*, 215.

point, more than two-thirds of all the manufacturing in America takes place outside city borders.[35]

There have always been dysgenic features of cities. The largely deteriorating city center served as one of the impetuses for suburbanization. Since then there have been ample efforts to rectify the problematic features via urban renewal projects to create vibrant neighborhoods with a walkable urbanism. It should come as no surprise that the suburbs and an auto-oriented lifestyle would also have adverse effects. Jeff Speck, in his chapter "Why Johnny Can't Walk" in *Walkable City* shows how a suburban car-oriented lifestyle leads to higher obesity rates, pollution, higher fatalities due to traffic accidents, and hypertension due to long commutes.

> According to the U.S. Centers for Disease Control (CDC), fully one-third of American children born after 2000 will become diabetics. This is due partly to diet, but partly to planning: the methodical eradication from our communities of the useful walk has helped create the least active generation in American history. The insult is compounded by the very real injuries that result from car crashes—the greatest killer of children and young adults nationwide—as well as an asthma epidemic tied directly to vehicle exhaust. Comparison of walkable cities and auto-dependent suburbs yields some eye-opening statistics—for example, that transit users are more than three times as likely as drivers to achieve their CDC-recommended thirty minutes of daily physical activity. Increasingly, it is becoming clear than the American healthcare crisis is largely an urban-design crisis, with walkability at the heart of the cure.[36]

---

[35] *The Great Inversion and the Future of the American City*, loc 1521.

[36] *Walkable City*, 38.

As a result, many are advocating that we need to curb sprawl, enhance walkability, and retrofit current suburbia. Diana Lind in "Cities Without Highways" states:

> Fortunately, there's another way. Think back to 1956: Sixty years later, most highways are reaching the end of their useful life. Elevated highways in particular are growing structurally obsolete, as cracks in concrete or faulty pillars can have easily disastrous consequences. This is an incredible opportunity to reshape the country's infrastructure in the face of metropolitan lifestyle that require more transit options and a different kind of housing stock.[37]

Harry Hiller notes that, "Advocates of urban sustainability propose to redesign the city and develop sustainable communities with more compact suburban development and mixed use that incorporates a range of housing and employment opportunities, the replacement of the automobile by transit, bicycles or walking, and a reduction in the ecological footprint of each household."[38]

Suburbanization in North America is a longstanding trend that has grown up (and out) in our cities. It has been woven into the urban fabric as long as people have been moving to cities and needing more space. One of the main catalysts that has allowed for explosive and expansive sprawl has indeed been the personal automobile. But now the questions are more along the lines of: What is the future of the suburbs? Can we retrofit the suburbs? How do we densify and

---

37 Lind, "Cities Without Highways," loc. 372.

38 *Urban Canada*, 219.

create walkability in the suburbs? Or as Jeff Mapes asks, "Can Americans really be seduced out of their cars in large numbers, at least for short trips?"[39]

This whirlwind trip down the suburban memory lane reveals only a cursory view of some of the issues and perspectives in which to view suburbanization. Most notably absent is a more robust conversation on race, neoliberal capitalism, postindustrialism, gender issues,[40] sexual orientation and housing,[41] environmental impacts, and so much more.[42] What this reveals is that addressing suburbanization is both complex and multi-faceted. It is more than a process brought on by a change in transportation technologies that accelerated the process, and more than merely what many Americans wanted. It was and is both, and so much more. The brevity of this chapter limits my ability to adequately address a wider range of perspectives, but there's enough from which to note some direct implications in regards to mission.

In 2011 I published *Metrospiritual: The Geography of Church Planting*. In the book, I studied church planting trends over the first decade of the 21st century. I tracked where new

---

[39] Mapes, *Pedaling Revolution*, 10.

[40] See Alison J. Clarke. "Tupperware: Suburbia, society and mass consumption." In *Visions of Suburbia*. New York: Routledge, 1996.

[41] See Sy Adler and Johanna Brenner. "Gender and Space: Lesbians and Gay Men in the City." In *The Urban Sociology Reader*, edited by Jan Lin and Christopher Mele, 200-207. New York: Routledge, 2012.

[42] See Becky Nicolaides and Andrew Wiese. *The Suburban Reader*. New York: Routledge, 2006.

churches were being planted across a multiplicity of denominations and church planting organizations in seven cities in the western half of the United States and Canada. The results revealed that roughly seventy percent of new churches were being started in the suburbs. A comparison with population dispersion also showed that roughly seventy percent of the population of these cities also lived in the suburbs. In other words, new churches were being started in direct proportion to where the bulk of the population lived.

However, as we explored in the last chapter, cities across the continent are continuously seeking to reinvent and reinvest in their city centers. Obviously some cities are further along than others, but the collective trend is that there is more interest not only in a revitalized urban core, but in general there is a growing desire to live an urban lifestyle. Based upon my observations in Portland and Vancouver, BC, as well as from stories I hear in cities across the country, there has been a distinctive shift in focus towards the central city not only in lifestyle preferences for Americans but in the location choices for new churches. In other words, if I were to redo my study now, what might it reveal? My guess is there would be a slight jump in the percentage of new churches being started in the central city than during the first decade of the century, but solid research would be needed to prove or disprove that hypothesis.

This then is a good place to pause and ask the question, "What is the future of suburbia?" As we have seen thus far, suburbia itself is not some monolithic phenomenon, but instead a complex and multi-layered way that cities have been and are growing outwards. But with fluctuating gas prices, global climate change, peak oil, and the push to create more sustainable cities, it is clear that suburbs will continue to transform. In their book *Retrofitting Suburbia,* authors Ellen Dunham-Jones and June Williamson point out three retrofitting strategies for the suburbs to consider:

- *Re-inhabitation.* The adaptive reuse of existing structures for more community-serving purposes, often as "third places" for social interaction.
- *Redevelopment.* Replacing existing structures and/or building on existing parking lots, generally with a compact, walkable, connected mix of uses and public spaces that supports a less auto-dependent and more socially engaged lifestyle.
- *Regreening.* Demolition of existing structures and revitalization of land, as either parks, community gardens, or reconnected wetlands. Regreening is sometimes a phasing strategy for eventual partial redevelopment.[43]

These strategies reflect creative and healthy ways to begin to curb sprawl, infill open spaces, creative a more activating walkable urbanism, and make suburban life overall more interconnected both physically and relationally. How could churches, whether established ones or new plants, participate in this endeavor in making the suburbs more relational and connected? This could be anything from making their church campuses more accessible and open to the public like allowing food carts in their mostly vacant parking lots. It could mean advocating for healthier and more sustainable development to encouraging more people to simply bicycle to their gatherings.

---

[43] Dunham-Jones and Williamson, *Retrofitting Suburbia*, viii.

In a lecture on "Next Generation Urbanism" at the Simon Fraser University Harbour Centre in Vancouver, BC, Duham-Jones asked a series of formative questions involving the future of suburbia:

- What kind of urbanism do we want?
- What kind of urbanism can we afford?
- What kind of city do we want?[44]

As was highlighted earlier in this chapter, numerous health and social factors are diminished when people live auto-based sedentary lives. In the same way, many urban areas adversely affected by crowded tenement buildings and a lack of basic amenities also had a negative impact on the populace. It was precisely these conditions that pushed for reform and which was also one of the catalysts for suburbanization as described in the works of Le Corbusier, Ebenezer Howard, or Frank Lloyd Wright. What kind of urbanism do we want? What kind of urbanism can we afford? What kind of city do we want?

How might the church and Christians help answer those questions and be stakeholders in the future of our cities? The Gospel is more than simply God's plan for redeeming our individual spiritual lives; in fact it includes everything ... the spiritual and the physical. In the same way, our urban communities, whether urban or suburban, are in need of Gospel transformation. How might we be the benefactors and curators of this process? Suburbanization truly has missiological implications. Encouraging a more sustainable,

---

[44] Dunham-Jones, "Next Generation Urbanism."

equitable, and walkable urbanism in the suburbs can directly impact social capital and thus create ripe conditions for new churches to be planted and for existing ones to grow.

What I would like to propose moves beyond the rote question of "what can we do to plant more churches?" Instead our question, which will be answered in completely different ways depending upon each particular setting, is, "How can the Gospel best be expressed for human flourishing?" Since the Gospel is the good news of the in-breaking Kingdom of God and redemption through Christ for the remission of our sins and the restoration of creation, then as ambassadors of this good news we have a lot of latitude for how we go about living that out. What does your suburb need for human flourishing? It could be more places for interconnectivity to raise the overall social capital (such as more public spaces); it could be new churches; or it could be more bike paths, better public transit, higher densities, better systems for newly arriving immigrants, more local businesses and less chain stores, and so much more. The possibilities are endless.

While suburbs may be an aberration in the historical development of cities, they are here to stay. Not only that, but there are many features of suburbia that are truly desirable to the majority of Americans whether it be space, affordability, or even its auto-centric lifestyle. That said, there are key attributes of suburbia that are not healthy nor sustainable over the long-term. Rather than being a passive observer to the changes in the urban fabric of our cities, what if Christians, both individually and collectively as churches, were to become part of shaping and reshaping the process of promoting more holistic, Gospel-centered human flourishing?

Chapter 4

Gentrification: Race, Economics, Housing, and Equity

Before delving into the topic of gentrification, which is certainly not a new topic in the literature of urban studies nor a new phenomenon, it is important that I declare my own intentions, biases, and even cultural framework in approaching this topic. First, the parts of the city I most enjoying living in are inner-city urban neighborhoods that are in transition. To be honest, living in a neighborhood such as the South Bronx when it bottomed-out and was burning, is not my default setting but I would not be opposed to it. At the same time, at the other end of the renewal spectrum, living in neighborhoods that have been thoroughly gentrified is not overly appealing to me, even though they definitely have elements that are desirous and enjoyable. In this I share some of the same sentiments as Sharon Zukin who laments whenever gritty urban neighborhoods become so gentrified (or yuppified) that they lose their "authenticity" as they transition into zones of cultural consumption. I enjoy the in-between places.

What I find fascinating about this in-between stage of gentrification is that these neighborhoods are in the midst of carving out their identities and figuring out who they are and what they will become. In the process of neighborhood succession, given the life-cycles of cities, there invariably will have been by now multiple transitions from one dominant ethnic group to another with more changes underway. From immigrant Italians to African-Americans to the next wave of neighborhood change through gentrification. What makes gentrification unique are all of the inequities associated with it. I am intrigued by these neighborhood changes. To me these conditions are ripe for the Gospel to be presented in a way that addresses such things as inequity and a civil society, and to define and redefine human flourishing.

There are elements of gentrification that I find fascinating, whether in watching neighborhood succession, the influx of new businesses catering to the creative class, changing amenities and services, and especially important to me, the renewal of existing churches and the planting of new ones.

I must also mark my own spot in the gentrification process. I am part of the white middle-class grouping known as the creative class in that I earn my living from knowledge-based or creative-based jobs. Church planters, I contend, are the creative class of the church. As entrepreneurs and cultural creatives, church planters engage daily in the process of creativity and innovation when it comes to communicating and embodying the Gospel. This is part of the reason for the draw of church planters into gentrifying neighborhoods. In light of that, thanks to my presence and cultural habits, it could be argued that I am part of the gentrification process. As

I ride through the neighborhood on my singlespeed bike or on my moped, I certainly if unintentionally look the part of the gentrifier even though I do not wish the negative or inequitable aspects of gentrification upon anyone.

One of the repercussions of urban ministry practitioners such as pastors, church planters, and the like moving into lower-income ethnic neighborhoods is that by their very presence they can act as catalysts of gentrification without meaning to. I have seen this take place all over the world as well-meaning and well-educated middle-class whites move into slums or inner-city ethnic neighborhoods to engage in ministry by loving the least, the last, and the lost. Churches, by the very nature of creating neighborhood stability and offering programs and assistance to long-standing residents to buy or fix up homes, create the conditions not only for gentrification, but they also send developers and investors the message that these neighborhoods are worthy of investment. So what is a church to do? How do churches and ministry leaders and practitioners navigate the terrain of gentrification to bring about a more Gospel-centered human flourishing?

My own cultural and ethnic blind spots mean that I am writing from the perspective of a middle-class white and that I look at the world through this lens. I cannot imagine what it was like to have my neighborhood redlined or to have my options for career, relocation, and education limited due to my ethnicity and where I grew up. This deeply pains me as I study American cities and see their gross inequities. I also know this grieves the heart of God who created us for a human flourishing that is both spiritual (because we are redeemed and reconciled to God through Christ), and cultural (because God set human flourishing in motion from the beginning ... the proliferation of the arts, humanities, sciences, equity, and so on).

When it comes to studying this phenomenon of gentrification, I appreciate Tom Slater's stance in his chapter "Gentrification of the City" in *The New Blackwell Companion to the City*. He advocates for viewing gentrification "from below."

> In particular I want to argue that a commitment to viewing the most serious consequence of gentrification—displacement—"from below" (i.e. in the terms of those who experience it) is essential if critical scholarship on gentrification is to overthrow the mainstream scholarship that does nothing more than parrot and perpetuate the status quo (widening class inequality in cities) with so much appeal to the media and to neoliberal policy elites.[1]

My hope and prayer is that through this chapter we can view gentrification from below, at the street level, and not from some lofty disengaged perch far above it all.

As I shared earlier, gentrification has been and is a topic of preeminent importance to me. There are a myriad of issues surrounding the topic which make it challenging and exciting to study and explore. There are numerous vantage points from which to address gentrification; economics (Fordism to Postfordism, creative or artisan), racial tensions, community development, housing, the gender and sexuality of the gentrifiers, bohemian culture, immigration, and so much more. Seemingly every time I peel back another layer I only

---

[1] Slater, "Gentrification of the City," 572.

discover infinitely more layers making the quest to know more about it never-ending.

I first became interested in gentrification when I worked as a Church Planting Strategist in Tucson, Arizona. Tasked with catalyzing new churches across the metro area I began to narrow my focus on the underserved urban neighborhoods and the downtown where there was an absence of new churches compared to the growing suburban fringe. As I immersed myself in the city I began tracking the beginnings of change in Tucson's downtown and various inner-city neighborhoods.

Over time I began to notice that church planters (at the time) were opting to start new churches on the suburban fringe. Conversely, degraded inner-city neighborhoods were being served by long-time established churches, most often mainline Protestant or Catholic churches who faithfully ministered to the changing neighborhood. At the same time I was refining the focus of my doctoral dissertation research at the seminary I was attending. My initial question as a Church Planting Strategist was, "Why are most of the new church plants located in the suburbs?" That question formed the trajectory of my research and dissertation under the guidance of Dr. Ron Boyce who helped me think through the geographic placement of churches in metro areas. I expanded my research focus to seven cities in the western half of the United States and Canada.

Of particular interest to me were new church plants that were being started in gentrifying neighborhoods. In my survey of nearly 230 new churches I had a second set of questions for those in these neighborhoods of transition. I wanted to know how they were responding to gentrification. Were they planting churches for the creative class or for the existing populace who tended to be lower-income minorities ... or both? Regardless of where new churches were being planted, I discovered that one of the primary motives for site selection among church planters was *homophily*.[2] Inevitably that meant if the church planter was white he planted churches in enclaves of white ethnicity, which in many cases tended to be suburban areas.[3] As cities revitalize and suburbs mature and change, this motivation is impacting where new churches are started, especially if the bulk of church planters still tend to be middle-class whites. Homophily is also one of the reasons why as inner-city Portland becomes whiter there are also more new churches being started. This all ties into the topic of gentrification as we begin pealing back the layers to try to understand it.

Scanning the literary landscape on the subject of gentrification is a painstakingly involved process. Where does one even begin? It is not a siloed conversation. Instead, it is a topic that is being addressed from a wide range of academic disciplines and perspectives from architecture to sociology to public policy to urban planning to community development to economics (be it on the macro or micro level) to housing— that barely scratches the surface. On top of that, how does the church planter enter into the conversation and on whose

---

[2] Benesh, *Metrospiritual*, 78.

[3] This is not a neat and tidy assertion. Books such as Ehrenhalt's *The Great Inversion and the Future of the American City* reveal the changing nature of suburbia.

behalf? The gentrifiers? The people already living in the neighborhood who could be displaced through gentrification?

It is a complex and multi-faceted topic. My purpose in this chapter, knowing that my audience most likely will be students, and urban ministry practitioners (pastors, church planters, professors, denominational leaders, etc.), is to give a broad overview of some of the processes and actors in gentrification. Again, this is only scratching the surface and is more of a primer to the conversation in order to stimulate further inquiry and exploration.[4]

For those living in cities this is a push-and-pull process that not only affects traditional inner-city neighborhoods, but has a direct bearing on the suburbs as well. In other words, regardless of where one lives in the city, all of the processes that create conditions ripe for gentrification are also influencing the city overall as it can lead to in-and-out migrations for various groups of people. The economic forces, whether deindustrialization, globalization, or the growing artisan economy, impact the outward and inward migration of people. Americans' changing cultural and neighborhood preferences also means that the classic demarcations of ethnic low-income inner-city neighborhoods and white homogenous suburbs will continue to change. Gentrification is not an isolated movement; it affects every urban dweller.

---

[4] I have another book that deals specifically with gentrification both from an academic, theological and a practitioner's perspective. I invited several others authors to contribute chapters whether scholarly works or stories of church planting in gentrifying neighborhoods. The book is called *Vespas, Cafes, Singlespeed Bikes, and Urban Hipsters: Gentrification, Urban Mission, and Church Planting*. Portland: Urban Loft, 2014.

In her 1964 essay on the changes taking place in London, Ruth Glass introduces the term "gentrification." "Once this process of gentrification starts in a district, it goes on rapidly until all or most of the original working class occupiers are displaced, and the whole social character of the district is changed."[5] Since that formative essay, the research and debate of gentrification has sped up and amplified. As Glass was observing the changes taking place in mid-century London, she identified multiple facets of the gentrification process.

So what is gentrification? Lees, Slater, and Wyly write that it is "the transformation of a working-class or vacant area of the central city into middle-class residential and/or commercial use."[6] Housing, neighborhood change, community development, and gentrification are all related and reveal different moving parts of the same dynamic forces and movements shaping neighborhoods and districts. The common storyline of neighborhood disinvestment is not only an economic conversation, but also deals specifically with housing and living conditions. Once an area has bottomed-out through capital disinvestment and the severing of local services, these areas become prime locales for reinvestment and rebirth. However, the rebirth or renewal process is complex with many actors and agencies playing a role.

---

[5] Glass, "Aspects of Change," 22-23.

[6] Lees et al., *Gentrification*, xv.

Bottoming Out, Housing Change, and the Economics of Gentrification

Detailing the story of the South Bronx in the twentieth century, chapter 2 ("Miracle on 174th Street") of *House by House, Block by Block* by Alexander von Hoffman revealed the story behind the Bronx's golden era, decline, bottoming out, and the beginning steps towards renewal. Since I write from the framework of having been involved in church planting and local church ministry for all of my post-college life, there were bits and pieces of this narrative that caught my attention. Most notably, it revealed some of the main actors who helped stabilize the neighborhood and turn it around. Von Hoffman notes that, "It was fitting that the religious clerics and faith-based organizations–of the type that President George W. Bush has championed–were prominent among those who spurred the revival."[7] My favorite part of the story was of Father Gigante, an Italian *mafioso-esque* Catholic priest, who once punched a politician during an argument. Despite his brash tactics, Gigante played an instrumental role in turning the community around.

House by House, Block by Block showcased the prominent role that housing plays in the process of urban decay, renewal, and gentrification. In many ways housing is the focal point. When the term "blight" is applied it most often is associated with housing. When gentrification is described it is most often associated with the middle-class moving into lower-income neighborhoods and fixing up the existing housing stock

---

[7] von Hoffman, *House by House, Block by Block*, 20.

97

whether it be brownstones or Victorians. This is also ground zero for the gentrification debates. Does gentrification really displace the poor as most assume? Some contend that gentrification *always* results in displacement but others contend that quite the opposite occurs.

Scholarship reveals that in some cases displacement does take place, but it should not be assumed as normative. Lance Freeman wrote an intriguing article entitled "Displacement or Succession? Residential Mobility in Gentrifying Neighborhoods," that argued against the displacement assumption. While Freeman concedes that indeed gentrification may cause displacement, he argues that the numbers are negligible or modest at best.[8] Lees et al echo Freeman and assert that, "Displacement is however, extremely difficult to quantify."[9] So the most controversial tenant of the backlash against gentrification, displacement, appears to be up for debate.

What is important to consider is that much of the debates about gentrification revolve around housing. That is not to be dismissive of the economic forces that shaped disinvestment in these same neighborhoods nor when they become ripe for reinvestment. In many ways housing and neighborhood succession is a surface level topic within gentrification because underneath the surface are other moving parts like globalization and the flow of capital. Disinvestment and reinvestment in housing are ultimately an economic

---

[8] Freeman, "Displacement of Succession?" 487-488.

[9] *Gentrification*, 218.

conversation. What then can the church do if gentrification is dictated by local as well as global economics?

It is oftentimes when neighborhoods are at their lowest that there are local advocates who will stand up to the landlords, judges, or other government officials on behalf of the poor. In many cases, as von Hoffman noted, this is where non-profits and churches step in. Wayne Gordon, former pastor of Lawndale Community Church in the Lawndale neighborhood of Chicago, has seen the neighborhood try to lift itself out of decay over the course of thirty-plus years. He talks about how the neighborhood "was a barren place lacking many of the services that a healthy community has."[10] Throughout his chapter in his book *A Heart for the Community* he wrestles with the pros and cons of gentrification. On the one hand, he writes, "Gentrification. A dreaded word to us in urban ministry and a major issue."[11] Later he admits that gentrification did indeed bring about a lot of good changes in the neighborhood. Instead of fighting it, he says we should work with it. "It is imperative for us not to see gentrification as the enemy but to embrace it."[12]

As a result. Lawndale Community Church started a community development agency. Through that they built hundreds of homes and helped many more people make down-payments on homes and offered classes to train people to be homeowners. Their church was helping stabilize and fix up the neighborhood, which ironically accelerated the process

---

[10] Gordon, "Gentrification," 41.

[11] Ibid., 39.

[12] Ibid., 47.

of gentrification. Gordon observes, "Actually we became a victim of our own success. As we were successful in building new houses, the market forces noticed us and began to work in our neighborhood."[13] In both Lawndale or the South Bronx, there arose advocates who did much of the dirty work of stemming the tide of decay and cleaning up the neighborhood. This then, as Gordon noted, helped catalyze the gentrification process.

So how then should churches in gentrifying neighborhoods act and respond? Or perhaps the better question is, what role should churches play in stabilizing neighborhoods that have bottomed-out in terms of disinvestment and "blight," even if they end up accelerating the gentrification process and thus displace the very ones they have been working with and helping out for years? Brent Toderian, in an article entitled, "Moving on From Gentrification to 'Shared Neighborhoods,'" contends that gentrification as a term may have lost its use. In essence, he says the word has become so emotionally charged that it is packed with (false) assumptions and oftentimes venom.

> Can you have revitalization, reinvestment, renewal without some level of gentrification? Probably not, as any perceived improvement in the eyes of the marketplace changes the economics. I do though, continue to believe that in planning for community change, there are reasonable levels of gentrification, that gentrification can be strategically managed, and that we can have "revitalization without displacement."[14]

---

[13] Ibid., 42.

[14] Toderian, "Moving on From Gentrification to 'Shared Neighborhoods,'" para. 2.

Replacement term

Instead, Toderan advocates using the term "shared neighbourhoods." He continues:

> Just as the "shared streets" movement has revolutionized (or just reintroduced) thinking around how walking, biking, transit and cars can all be accommodated within street design, a "shared neighbourhoods" approach would emphasize adding more diverse population and uses into neighborhoods without displacement of those most vulnerable. This isn't replacement,—it's renewal where the whole new neighborhood is welcomed and accommodated.[15]

Maybe there can be a healthy dose of gentrification without the negative repercussions. Certainly, no one is longing for these "good ol' days" when the South Bronx was burning due to arson and neglect. The question becomes whether we can truly have neighborhood change without displacing most of the current populace. Also, not everyone who moved into formerly disinvested neighborhoods had dubious or ulterior motives. They simply wanted an inexpensive place to live. In fact, some even moved into these neighborhoods in turmoil because in some way they were seeking safe havens from conservative middle-class suburbs.

When urban neighborhoods are vulnerable their housing is cheap. One person's blight is another person's refuge. Those escaping various forms of oppression find a welcome home in the neighborhood despite the decay. These "pioneer gentrifiers" come in various forms ranging from artists, speculators, developers, to the gay community. "Researchers

---

[15] Ibid., para. 8.

have also noted the emancipatory qualities of the inner city for the gay community."[16] In the chapter "Gender and Space: Lesbians and Gay Men in the City," authors Sy Adler and Johanna Brenner also note this trend: "While 'property, family, and wealth' are barriers to lesbian settlements, counter-cultural neighborhoods appear to be most open."[17] These can take the form of bohemian enclaves (i.e., gentrifying or "pre-gentrifying" neighborhoods). Gentrifying neighborhoods, in the midst of much transition, tend to be a favorable and tolerant landing place whether for lesbians, gays, or different ethnicities. As a result, many are drawn to gentrifying neighborhoods. For some, then, gentrification is viewed as negative while for others it is a process of hope, renewal, and new opportunities. Again, how is the church to respond?

What this reveals is there are multiple actors and processes involved in the gentrification process, from housing to economic factors (locally and globally) to emancipatory motives to lifestyle preference and racism, to name a few. Many others are motivated to move into inner-city urban neighborhoods simply because of the appeal of living in historic old buildings. In other words, it is precisely the gritty characteristics of these neighborhoods that attracts them. Sharon Zukin, in "The Creation of a 'Loft Lifestyle'" writes:

> Because the middle class generally neither inherits baronial ancestral halls nor can afford to reconstruct such palaces, the housing that the middle class builds or buys

---

[16] *Gentrification*, 213.

[17] Adler and Brenner, "Gender and Space," 205.

necessarily reflects new ideas about space, and what is represents, in each time period. In that sense, loft living is part of a larger modern quest for authenticity. Old buildings and old neighborhoods are "authentic" in a way that new construction and new communities are not. They have an identity that comes from years of continuous use, and an individuality that creates a sense of 'place' instead of place."[18]

Tim Butler echoes Zukin when he too observes people moving into old urban neighborhoods because of their style and attractiveness. "Oldness, or images of oldness, are important to a new class that is trying to emphasise its 'place' in the social structure."[19] Through interviews with middle class Londoners who moved back into the old central city, Butler discovered multiple reasons why these people made the move. Surprisingly, the motives were not that dubious: they wanted shorter work commutes and affordable housing that they could fix up. He even notes, "The desire to live in an old house emerges as a powerful reason for living in the inner city."[20]

What this reveals is that the process of gentrification is not uniform in the sense that all of the gentrifiers are "bad" people looking to kick out low-income minorities. They are moving into inner cities because for numerous positive reasons. As our economies grow and capital becomes more mobile, more people will have the ability to live where they want to.

---

[18] Zukin, "The Creation of a 'Loft Lifestyle," 181.

[19] Butler, "Consumption and Culture," 236.

[20] Ibid., 248.

While the racial dynamics of gentrification are what garner most of the attention, as well as the outrage, underneath it all are the ever-changing local and global economies that keep moving many of the pieces around. This is where the gentrification conversation turns to addressing the economic dynamics and factors at play. In a *Relevant Magazine* article called "Pushing City Limits," Emily Miller writes, "The process [of gentrification] often begins when artists looking for cheap rent migrate into low-income neighborhoods. This hipster influx brings fresh vitality to the neighborhood, which yuppie urbanites soon begin to see as cultural hotspots rather than the 'bad side of town' it once was."[21] This is precisely the process that Richard Lloyd describes in *Neo-Bohemia* as he recounts the transition and transformation of Wicker Park in Chicago from a blue-collar immigrant community to a hipster and bohemian enclave.

While gentrification is about housing, Lloyd contends it is also about economics and the changing forces of a shift to post-Fordism. "The dynamic shifts in the local economy and demography are embedded in social processes that are global in scope, including displacement of manufacturing from old urban centers to suburban locales and, later, to sites outside the United States."[22]

Gottdiener and Hutchinson look at the impact of the global economy on the process of suburbanization in their chapter "Suburbanization, Globalization, and the Emergence of the Multicentered Region." Why talk about

---

[21] Miller, "Pushing City Limits," para. 6.

[22] Lloyd, *Neo-Bohemia*, 25.

suburbanization in a chapter on gentrification? As you will see, the global economic forces that created the conditions for gentrification also impacted suburbanization. This global economy, which accelerated from the 1960s onwards, had an impact on suburbanization here. "The United States began to lose jobs to locations outside the country as labor sourcing led corporations to set up shop in countries where wages were considerably lower and workers were considerably more docile than in America. This process is known as deindustrialization and it has led over the decades to a massive decline in manufacturing within the United States."[23] This global reshuffling sped up the process of suburbanization. As city centers hollowed out due to factories closing down and moving overseas, as Lloyd noted in *Neo-Bohemia*, it resulted in economic disinvestment, joblessness in central cities, which in turn had a reciprocal affect on the social fabric of cities. Things went from bad to worse, and it could be argued that globalization played an instrumental role in the process as many central city residents fled to the suburbs.

Suburbanization, while accelerated by changing transportation technologies and middle-class cultural appeal, went definitively into overdrive through globalization. We can see this impact in former manufacturing powerhouses like Cleveland and Detroit. Globalization decimated these cities and most notably their central cities as jobs were moved overseas or to the suburbs or to Sunbelt cities in search of cheaper (and non-unionized) labor and cheaper space. Other manufacturing plants simply closed down because they were

---

[23] Gottdiener and Hutchinson, *The New Urban Sociology*, 130.

unable to compete with the lower costs elsewhere in the emerging global economy. Pittsburgh, as an example, was once an industrial city with 32 percent of its workforce engaged in manufacturing. By the 1980s that had fallen to just 5.5 percent.[24]

On the heels of this hollowing out many lower-income residents, including many ethnic minorities, continued to move into these very same neighborhoods because they were affordable. On the one hand the trajectory of decline was already firmly established. And yet capital reinvestment into these same neighborhoods runs parallel to gentrification; these processes are interwoven. As a result, gentrification is more than housing and displacement, it is also reflective of a changing economy and the imminent altering of culture which sees these old urban neighborhoods more favorably.

What this Means for the Church

Late last night I flew back to Portland after spending a few days in Fort Worth, Texas. Specifically I had been in the Near Southside neighborhood on the southern flank of the city's central business district. It and those around it have gone through various cycles of growth over the past century to a time of decline as people moved out to the suburbs to its current state of economic reinvestment and interest in the neighborhood. The purpose of my trip was the facilitate a Gentrification Studio with church leaders ministering in the heart of this rapidly changing neighborhood.

---

[24] Ibid., 131.

It is a neighborhood in transition. Year by year more and more signs of turnaround are popping up from coffee roasters to breweries to bike lanes to green infrastructure and more. One of the unique facets of this neighborhood is the relatively small residential population. While anchored by numerous medical institutions (hospitals, clinics, etc.) most of the rest of the neighborhood is a patchwork of vacant lots, new and old businesses, and sporadic new residential housing catering to the medical professions and those who work downtown. On one street is Section 8 housing across the road from new condos or apartments.

While it is not a typical gentrifying neighborhood, it is gentrification nonetheless. Called *new build gentrification* or *brownfield gentrification* since most of the neighborhood is *not* full of houses, it still has much of the same attributes ... middle-class people moving in, capital flowing back into the neighborhood, increased services and amenities, and so on. This has caused housing costs to increase not only in the immediate neighborhood but in the adjoining neighborhoods as well.

The big questions before us at the Studio were ... *How do we respond? How should churches respond to gentrification in their neighborhood? And how should individuals living in the heart of the city also respond?* Since every city and neighborhood going through gentrification is unique, then each response will be just as unique and contextualized. That means each and every church and church plant, as well as every Christian living in these neighborhoods and districts, will have their own unique response depending on the make-up of their neighborhood and church.

The goal of the Studio was to facilitate conversations about gentrification and then lead the group through developing their own *implementation plan.* You see, while there are common characteristics of gentrification taking place in all settings, as I say, each place and each church is unique. I don't prescribe plans for these group to adopt. I simply educate and facilitate, and walk them through developing a "now what?" response. After two days of teaching, talking, exploring, and city tours how then should they practically and tangibly respond? That is what the Gentrification Studio is about.

Churches and individuals care deeply about this topic and with coming up with helpful ways to respond. On the first night of the Studio we met at Chimera Brewing on Magnolia Avenue outside on the back patio. It became a "public" gathering. Surrounded by other picnic tables and people constantly coming and going meant that at times people would stop and listen. At one point we had a drunk woman join our group. She was actually fully engaged in the conversation and contributed a lot to it. Her F-bomb-filled insights were spot-on.

Later on a young business professional joined us and seemed intrigued by our conversation. The next day when we met at Brewed just a few blocks away he stopped by on his lunch break. Both of these people were upfront in self-identifying as non-Christians, but they were incredibly interested in the conversation and appreciative that our group cared enough to get together to talk about gentrification. Gentrification is an issue that many are interested in, whether they're inside the church or not. The bottom line is that we need to respond in helpful and life-giving ways. That includes partnering with entities, organizations, and individuals outside of the church to try to bring about a more hopeful future for these neighborhoods.

So where does this conversation leave us in light of the scope of the book and church planting in the city? Just like the Gentrification Studio process that I mentioned above, I don't prescribe any formulas or prescriptions. Every city is different, every neighborhood is unique, and every church planter core team is called, gifted, and hard-wired to respond accordingly. If they're a talented group of artists, artisans, or musicians, the response will look vastly different from a group with backgrounds in business, real estate, or urban development. Not surprisingly, since bicycles and creative start-ups are my hobbies and passions, it makes sense that I view gentrification through the grid of transportation, mobility, and the local creative or artisan economy.

Your response is not only something you need to pray through with your team, you also need take a deeper look at who you are, how you are wired, the experiences the Lord has brought you through, what you're gifted in, your passions, because all of this will affect the outcomes of how you are to live out the Gospel in gentrifying neighborhoods. In other words, there are a myriad ways to respond to gentrification. But common to all of them are: Investigate. Explore. Pray. Act.

Chapter 5

The Artisan Economy, Creative Class, and Church Planting

Portland is an amazing city to live in, visit, and watch hipsters and bohemians in their natural habitat. As I explain to out-of-town visitors, while other cities have their hipster enclaves, Portland is one enormous hipster city. For many reasons, Portland's fame continues to spread and grow. It's not simply for its weirdness that the city's brand reaches far and wide. There are numerous movements, trends, and phenomena all coalescing in this city at once that have created an environment for all sorts of things to grow and flourish. It is a city of extremes. Two days ago over ten thousand nude cyclists paraded through the downtown with the streets lined with thousands of ogling onlookers. Yes, it was a legal event. At the other end of the spectrum, it is a city which contains a surprisingly high number of evangelical colleges, universities, seminaries, and ministries. Hopefully the latter were not riding through town with the former.

As the only major American city which has a *platinum-level* designation for being a bike-friendly community, Portland is becoming an ever-increasingly popular travel destination. But one of the markers that makes Portland unique among other cities is the undercurrent of its economy which certainly can be called *Post-Fordist*. But which came first? The artisans (bohemians, hipsters, creative class) or *Post-Fordism*? In this chapter I will walk through the development of the whole artisan economy, which includes a conversation about Fordism vs. Post-Fordism.

Portland, like many other American cities, has seen an uptick in people moving back into the central city. For example, the Pearl District, located in Portland's downtown core, as recently as the 1990s was a sketchy and unsafe warehouse district when the first wave of gentrifiers were coming in. Mostly they were artists looking for cheap studio and gallery space. Some supposedly said that these studios and galleries were like "pearls" amidst the "crusty oysters" of the dilapidated surrounding warehouses and light-industrial buildings. That off-hand remark stuck and today it is officially known as the Pearl.

Economist Richard Florida notes the growing allure of urban central cities and the reverse-migration as people are moving back in:

> Several forces have combined to bring people and economic activity back to urban areas. First, crime is down and cities are safer. Second, cities have become the prime location for the creative lifestyle and the new amenities that go with it. Third, cities are benefiting from powerful demographic shifts. With fewer people living as married couples and more staying single longer, urban areas serve as lifestyle centers and as mating markets for single people. Fourth, cities have reemerged as centers of creativity and incubators of innovation. High-tech

companies and other creative endeavors continue to sprout in urban neighborhoods that we once had written off, in cities from New York to Chicago to Boston. Fifth, the current round of urban revitalization is giving rise to serious tensions between established neighborhood residents and newer, more affluent people moving in. Finally, in one of the most ironic twists in recent memory, both sprawling cities and traditional suburbs are seeking to emulate elements of urban life.[1]

The significance of this in relation to our conversation at hand is that those who are moving in are often associated with bohemians, artisans, hipsters, and the creative class. As time passes, what has become abundantly clear is that cities are pulling out all the stops to attract and retain these neo-bohemians. "Cities around the world are in competition with one another to attract and serve knowledge workers in the new economy and professional and managerial classes through entertainment districts and the arts, loft and luxury condominium developments in downtown core, and high-tech industrial parks on the exurban fringe."[2] The irony is that bohemians were once a marginalized class of people in European cities and now they are the poster-children of hip and trendy urban districts.

---

[1] Florida, *Rise of the Creative Class*, 287-90.

[2] Hiller, *Urban Canada*, 212.

The Rise of the Creative Class

One of the identifying markers of this burgeoning creative class is that they gain their livelihood through their intellect and creativity. Yes, these are broad and very wide categories. However, this is and continues to be a decisive shift away from the more blue-collar manufacturing economy that is part of Fordism. The reality is that this creativity comes in many shapes, forms, and expressions. Since Portland is a poster-child for this new growing class and economy then certainly we will find ample examples of these types throughout the city. "Other cities have their bohemian districts, but Portland stands alone as an urban economy that has broadly embraced the artisan approach to living and working. Scholars including Elizabeth Currid, Richard Lloyd, and Richard Florida have told parts of the story of arts economies and the creative class, but it all comes together here in Portland."[3]

Portland's artisan economy is unique on many fronts. I know countless people who walked away from corporate careers and ladder-climbing to either move to Portland or simple branch out into something that was more meaningful and creative. Not too long ago I had a conversation with the owner of a local coffee roaster who did just that, walked away from his downtown corporate job. His business' big Portland schtick is that they deliver all of their coffee by cargo bike. (They have one of the coolest cargo bikes I have ever seen.) Another friend of mine moved to Portland from the east coast after earning two degrees from prestigious universities including a degree in environmental law and policy. He

---

[3] Heying, *Brew to Bikes*, 17.

moonlights as a project manager for a new bicycle pathway project, but also spends countless hours each week as a cycling guide. In this latter gig he is a master storyteller recounting the history of Portland to bicycle tourists.

So who is this nebulous creative class? Richard Florida writes:

> The distinguishing characteristic of the Creative Class is that its members engage in work whose function is to "create meaningful new forms" define the Creative Class as consisting of two components. The Super-Creative Core of this new class includes scientists and engineers, university professors, poets and novelists, artists, entertainers, actors, designers and architects, as well as the thought leadership of modern society: nonfiction writers, editors, cultural figures, think-tank researchers, analysts and other opinion-makers. Whether they are software programmers or engineers, architects or filmmakers, they fully engage in the creative process.[4]

Within this creative class there is also a larger over-arching category.

> Beyond this core group, the Creative Class also includes "creative professionals" who work in a wide range of knowledge-intensive industries such as high-tech sectors, financial services, the legal and health care professions, and business management. These people engage in creative problem solving, drawing on complex bodies of knowledge to solve specific problems. Doing so typically requires a high degree of formal education and thus a high level of human capital.[5]

---

[4] *The Rise of the Creative Class*, 69.

[5] Ibid.

Fordism and Post-Fordism

The conversation about bohemians, hipsters, artisans, and the creative class is in actuality an economic conversation, because what separates them and makes them stand out is really their jobs and careers. It also gets back to the question of which came first. Does this class of people create an artisan economy, or does this economic reality create artisans?

Henry Ford had a significant impact upon American culture. While he did not invent the automobile, he made sure that every American had the opportunity to buy one. Through creative genius, innovation, and determination he figured out how to mass produce cars using an assembly line. This means of mass production has been dubbed "Fordism." "Fordism refers to the economic and institutional forms that became dominant in the late nineteenth century and reaches maturity in the post-World War II period. It is an economic system organized around mass production and mass consumption, and is so named because important aspects of the revolutionary restructuring of economic organization were introduced Henry Ford."[6] Numerous attributes of Fordism have become synonymous with the American manufacturing economy:

- The standardization of the product (nothing hand-made: everything is made through machines, molds and not by skilled craftsmanship).
- The use of special-purpose tools and/or equipment designed to make assembly lines possible: tools are

---

[6] *Brew to Bikes*, 23.

designed to permit workers with low skill levels to operate "assembly lines"—where each worker does one task over and over and over again—like on a doll assembly line, where one worker might spend all day every day screwing on doll heads.

- Workers are paid higher "living" wages, so they can afford to purchase the products they make.
- Other characteristics of the Fordist system are huge manufacturing complexes that anchor the urban economies of iconic locations such as Detroit and employ large numbers of unionized laborers who expect to be working for the company through most of their employed lifetimes.[7]

Fordism celebrates uniformity, standardization, and consistency. A McDonald's cheeseburger must taste the same in Seattle or Miami or Moscow. A venti iced chai at Starbucks ought to taste the same in Dallas or Detroit or Dubai. On the surface that's a good thing and makes a lot of sense. Regardless of what month in which we purchase a new car, everything about it should be the same. It would not quite work to have a "bad batch" of Ford Fiestas in February, but followed by a "great batch" in March and August. There must be consistently high standards throughout. To fail at that would jeopardize the whole system, or at least cost the company millions in recalls.

Workers in Fordist enterprises do not necessarily need to be skilled or educated. Maybe all they do is pull a lever all day, eight hours a day, forty hours a week. Their role is part of the larger assembly line. They may be placing a key component or part on an automobile, digital device, or bicycle, but know

---

[7] Ibid., 24.

little about the overall process or the mechanics of how the whole thing works. They simply pull their lever.

Beyond creating uniformity in a product, Fordism has also created uniformity in mass cultural consumption. Most popular music or movies fit into this genre of products that are mass-produced for cultural consumption. Just because an album is a best-seller does not always mean that it's the highest quality music; it is simply popular because its creators know what will appeal to the largest audience. It's the same with mainstream movies. We have become consumers of mass culture. It is a shared narrative regardless of where one lives. It is a global phenomenon.

Bohemians and Post-Fordism

Parallel with the Fordism narrative is Post-Fordism. Charles Heying calls it the *Artisan Economy*. It's not really a new storyline, and nor will it replace Fordism. But as Fordism has crept into so many facets of society and the global culture, there has arisen a backlash of sorts. A growing group of people, disenfranchised by the excesses of Fordism, are opting in favor of this alternative narrative. People want to be more in tune and in touch with what they are buying or consuming. In the first episode of the first season of the popular TV show *Portlandia*, one of the sketches displays, with Portland-food-fetish-fanaticism, the importance of knowing where the chicken they are about to eat comes from.

People want to be more intimately involved in the process and even production of what they use and consume. Rather than walking down the endless aisles of a national chain grocery store to purchase mass-produced food, more and more people are either now buying locally-sourced food or growing their own. This is one place where Post-Fordism intersects with neo-bohemians, hipsters, and the creative class.

"Post-Fordism describes the phase shift in the market/industrial system in which the success and contradictions of the Fordist system are resolved in new set of economic and institutional relationships. The watershed of this period of crisis and transformation is generally set around 1970."[8] Like Fordism, there are associated attributes that define this growing economic force.

- Small-batch production.
- Specialized products and jobs.
- New information technologies.
- Emphasis on types of consumers in contrast to the previous emphasis on social class.
- The rise of the service-industry and white-collar worker.
- The feminization of the work force.[9]

What becomes immediately noticeable is the scale of output. From large quantity to small-batch. However, this list represents only the beginning. The table on the next page taken from *Brew to Bikes* details in more vivid detail the stark contrast between Fordism and Post-Fordism.[10] It should also be noted that these are only a select number of the attributes listed there.

---

[8] Ibid., 25.

[9] Wikimedia Foundation, Inc., "Post-Fordism"

[10] *Brew to Bikes*, 54-55.

Artisan Economy	Fordist Economy
Product Qualities	
Handmade	Standardized
Similar but not uniform	Obsessive uniformity
Variation is appreciated	Low tolerance for variation
Authentic	Faux
Locally distinct	Universal, generic
Work Life	
Improvisational work	Routine work
Work as vocation	Work for pay
Work follows rhythms of season, project	Work times fixed and monitored
Integration of work, living, socializing spaces	Segregation of work, living, socializing spaces
Organizational Structure	
Small and medium scale enterprise	Large scale enterprise
Higher work autonomy	Low worker autonomy
Clustered, collaborative firms	Hierarchically organized firms
Moral Economy	
Less is more	Structural imperative for growth
Reinvestment in social and ecological infrastructure	Exploitation of social and ecological infrastructure

Post-Fordism and the City

"As urban economies shifted from Fordist industrial production to post-Fordist knowledge, and service industries and globalization increased competition between cities, a consensus developed that central cities had increasingly become sites of consumption rather than production."[11] That observation is pivotal to understanding the creative class and artisan church planting. The geography of the artisan economy is concentrated in inner-city urban contexts. That is coupled with the reality that the highest concentrations of neo-bohemians and the creative class are located in these same districts and neighborhoods.

There is a new pecking order among cities that reflects this reality. Central cities that are being revitalized (and gentrified) are seeing an increase in not only neo-bohemians, but in new artisan start-ups as well. This bodes well for these reemerging neighborhoods in terms of economic viability. "To attract these high-income workers and the footloose new-economy industries to the city, many urban policymakers focus their entrepreneurial efforts on remaking the city into what Lloyd and Clark label 'an Entertainment Machine.'"[12] Heying adds, "Cities that have the cultural ambiance that resonates with the creative class will enter into a virtuous cycle of growth, attracting or growing clusters of new-economy

---

[11] Ibid., 27.

[12] Ibid.

industries that, in turn, become thick with opportunity and possibility for change."[13]

What this does is elevate the importance of place, and in central cities in particular. These places are the habitat of hipsters. As a result, this is an economic conversation in that cities are now seeking to woo this elusive creative class. This is more important than perhaps many realize.

The creative class approach, in essence, is that a city's success hinges on the presence of the knowledge workers, the white-collar, cultural creatives. "[Richard] Florida's central thesis, therefore, is that a city's economic success may depend markedly on its ability to attract and retain members of the Creative Class."[14] City after city across the United States and Canada has bought into this rhetoric and begun reinvesting in and regenerating their central cities. Even old northern cities that were once the epicenter of industrialization are shedding old labels in favor of enticing the creative class back into their declining downtowns. Florida points out that this very strategy is alive and working even in cities like Detroit. "Thousands of residents, including designers, techies and music makers, have moved to Detroit's old central business district. They are drawn, to borrow a phrase from Jane Jacobs' 1961 work, *The Death and Life of Great American Cities*, to the old buildings new ideas require."[15]

---

[13] Ibid., 29.

[14] Ibid.

[15] Florida, "Detroit Shows Way to Beat Inner City Blues," para, 3.

But not everyone is drinking Florida's Kool-Aid. After his book *The Rise of the Creative* was released in 2002 there was a backlash among scholars who derided his allegedly weak analysis and contrived conclusions.[16] As Markusen points out, part of the dissonance is how Florida lumps together various industries which may or may not be reflective of truly "creative" jobs:

> Florida's creative class groupings are based on major occupational groups—he does not look inside each of these to see what they contain. Business and financial occupations, for instance, include claims adjusters and purchasing agents. Managers include sales and food-service managers and funeral directors. Computer and mathematical occupations include actuaries and tax collectors. Engineers include surveyors and drafting technicians. Health care practitioners include dental hygienists and dietary and pharmacy technicians. These occupations may indeed be creative, but so too are airplane pilots, ship engineers, millwrights, and tailors— all of whom are uncreative in Florida's tally. The discussion of the creative class is fudged yet more by Florida's selective use of interviews and anecdote to suggest behaviors and preferences that are not representative of the "class" as a whole.[17]

Regardless, cities from Portland to St. Louis to Milwaukee to Brooklyn have bought into this creative economy and its creative class as a strategy for urban regeneration.

---

[16] Markusen, "Urban Development and the Politics of a Creative Class," 1922.

[17] Ibid., 1923.

Arts and the City

Any discussion of the creative class quickly branches out into other topics and fields such as art, culture, tourism, and regeneration. The very nature of the term "creative" brings with it an affirmation of the arts. If a city is to experience a flourishing of the arts then what role do artists themselves play? Are they homegrown or are they outsiders who've been drawn to a city that is "happening?" Is the burgeoning arts scene a strategic economic and cultural initiative undertaken to shift a city away from manufacturing to hi-tech, white collar, and more creative or knowledge-based jobs? Along with those initial questions there are bound to be a myriad more as the conversation can quickly turn to the creative class theory, how cities are all-in on this socio-economic grouping, and the resultant impact of gentrification and urban revitalization.

Narrowing the conversation of the creative class specifically to artists, Elizabeth Currid asks, "How do we create places where talented people, who are footloose, capricious, and in high demand, want to live and work? What sort of place-based characteristics do they seek out?"[18]

One of the key components of the creative economy that Currid explores in her article "How Art and Culture Happen in New York" reveals that agglomeration is key to the success and vibrancy of a city's art scene, "Planners and economic developers have long noted that clustering like-minded firms, labor pools, institutions, and resources is important to transferring information, supplies, and ideas efficiently,

---

[18] Currid, "How Art and Culture Happen in New York," 454.

resulting in localized economic benefits. Agglomeration may be even more important to maintaining the social mechanisms by which the cultural economy sustains itself."[19] The appeal to planners and developers then is that if a city can gather its share of cultural creatives by proximity the benefits of agglomeration multiply. This bodes well for a city's outlook in terms of the arts and ultimately its creative or artisan economy.

One of the challenges of cities that cater to the creative class, as Currid has noted, is that while they can serve as catalysts for urban regeneration, their efforts in the end can have the adverse impact of pricing themselves out of the very neighborhoods they moved into. The artists who create these desirable locations can only watch as non-artists move in and drive up housing costs thus driving out the very ones who helped turn neighborhoods around.[20]

Creative Economies and Urban Regeneration

Artists living in cities have been noted to favor more authentic gritty neighborhoods. Their motives range from aesthetic preference to simply the low cost of spaces in urban neighborhoods on the decline. These neighborhoods often have ample housing and studio stock for artists to move into and utilize. It could be argued that in some ways these kinds of places serve as "canvases" for artists and cultural creatives to fashion and frame space in the city. The potency is that for cities image is everything. In the minds of planners, mayors,

---

[19] Ibid., 460.

[20] Ibid., 463.

and developers, the image of their city projects can either hurt or help their economic outlook. "[The] cultural power to create an image, to frame a vision, of the city has become more important as publics have become more mobile and diverse, and traditional institutions—both social classes and political parties—have become less relevant mechanisms of expressing identity."[21]

The power of image was the driving force behind Milwaukee's insistence on throwing their lot in with the creative class and Richard Florida's theories for economic transformation. Once defined as a manufacturing-based city built on shipping and brewing, Milwaukee, like many other northern cities, had lost a considerable number of manufacturing jobs and families. This spurred on civic leaders to bring in Florida to consult with them about their future and what to do to get there. Jeffrey Zimmerman writes,

> Having apparently realized that their city will never be a truly global place, and that the factories and middle-class families are never coming back, Milwaukee's growth coalitions are now striking out more modestly, hoping to successfully compete for a larger share of the region's young and college-educated. The city's new thinking is rooted precisely in Florida's theory of urban growth, which maintains that the presence of a large creative class produces economic prosperity in the new economy in the long run.[22]

---

[21] Zukin, "Whose Culture? Whose City?" 283.

[22] Zimmerman, "From Brew Town to Cool Town," 231.

Zimmerman details how civic leaders bought into Florida's ideal and poured hundreds of millions of dollar into urban regeneration projects in the city center while, for example, in 2006 closing 90 percent of the city's swimming pools due to "budget shortfalls."[23] That was only the tip of the iceberg. "Nearly eight years into its creative city development experiment, Milwaukee remains a city in deep, and rapidly intensifying, socioeconomic trouble."[24] It could very well be that Milwaukee's Achilles' heel was that for them it became either/or rather than both/and. That's to say, while the city began disregarding and downplaying its traditional manufacturing economy it was undercutting its roots and the economy that built the city. "The substantive hallmark of Milwaukee's Florida-inspired municipal action therefore was an approximately $300 million public subsidy directed at pampering the professional classes and lubricating their continued resettlement from one part of the metropolitan area to another."[25]

Instead of creating an either/or dichotomy, Donegan et al instead affirm cities buying into the creative class and yet simultaneously continuing to build and invest in their traditional manufacturing economy. "Our empirical analysis of Florida's creativity measures, however, leads us to conclude that attracting the creative class is no substitute for traditional strategies such as investing in quality education, upgrading the

---

[23] Ibid., 241.

[24] Ibid., 240.

[25] Ibid.

skills of the workforce, creating new businesses, or expanding existing industries."[26] They even argue that the presence of the creative class is not a disadvantage to cities, but needs to be coupled with a both/and approach. While creative class strategies are instrumental in a city's future, including urban regeneration projects like infill and waterfront redevelopment, it does not need to come at the exclusion of buttressing a city's working class economy.

The Built Environment and the Creative Class

When it comes to the urban fabric of cities the built environment is a key component to attracting the creative class. With Donegan et al, I affirm this notion of being both/ and when it comes to an urban economic focus. Besides, classic demarcations of the stereotypes of the creative class are simply an overgeneralized caricature that resembles everyone and yet no one at the same time. As an example, *Bike Portland* recently did a feature article on bicycle commuters and bike parking at the Swan Island Industrial Park. This industrial hub in Portland does not represent Florida's creative class. At the same time, burly middle-aged men in plaid on bikes do not resemble the popular image of a Portland bicycle commuter.[27] Nonetheless, these people and industries play a key role in the

---

[26] Donegan et al., "Which Indicators Explain Metropolitan Economic Performance Best?" 192.

[27] Maus, "Daimler Trucks North America opens new bike parking facility on Swan Island."

city's economic future which is why the both/and motif is vital.

If we're going to be all-in with the creative class (and simultaneously all-in with traditional industries) then I am in favor of creating certain kinds of conditions in the built environment that accentuate the creative class. In a *Wall Street Journal* article, Florida asks, "Over the next 50 years we will spend trillions of dollars on city building. The question is: How should we build?"[28] Florida goes on to talk about density and its affect on a city's "metabolism."

> Look at New York City. Its hubs of innovation aren't the great skyscraper districts that house established corporate and financial headquarters, media empires and wealthy people (an increasing number of whom are part-time residents who hail from the ranks of the global super-rich). The city's recent high-tech boom—500 start-ups in the last half decade, among them Kickstarter and Tumblr —is anchored in mid-rise, mixed-use neighborhoods like the Flatiron District, Midtown South, Chelsea and TriBeCa."[29]

If we're deploying a both/and strategy, then making sure that a city has ample districts and neighborhoods that are creative class-friendly is certainly a worthy investment.

---

[28] Florida, "To Build Creative Cities, the Sky Has Its Limits," para, 2.

[29] Ibid., para. 10.

A Call for an Artisan Approach to Church Planting

This journey through the artisan economy and creative class has significant missiological implications, especially as it pertains to the starting of new churches. This crystallized for me when I was teaching a seminary course on the Introduction to Church Planting. Rather than teaching through the conventional thinking on church planting (e.g., core group, launch, marketing, etc.) I spent several class periods talking about urban economics and the rise of the creative class. With the same chart that I have included in this chapter up on the screen, we compared and contrasted what church planting could look like under the motif of Post-Fordism (Artisan) versus Fordism. It was a lively discussion.

I would contend that most church planting today and over the past several decades has been thoroughly Fordist in approach. If we note the chart comparing the characteristics of the Fordist Economy with the Artisan Economy we would see church planting as being standardized, uniform, universal, with low levels of variation, work for pay, and hierarchical organizations, to name a few. Welcome to the way we do church planting today ... it's Fordist. Even our training mechanisms, whether denominational or through a church planting network, are uniform and standardized regardless of the context of where one is planting a church.

If we were to look at the measurables and the hoped-for or assumed results they too are uniform and universal. They are void of the contextual realities even if one is planting in a church-saturated culture or among the urban poor or in a post-Christian urban gentrifying setting; the results and the measurables are still the same. Most often church planters themselves are held to the same standards. In terms of work for pay, they probably cringe at that. I have sat through meetings where denominations have cut funding for planters in order to incentivize them to produce more so they can be rewarded with more money. I even saw a chart where if the planter got his church up to a certain number of people then his pay would increase by a corresponding amount, and so forth.

improper metrics

What would church planting look like under the framework of the Artisan Economy? What can Portland, which is a hotbed for this burgeoning creative class, teach us about church planting and the passion for Gospel-centered innovation? My motivation in pushing this conversation forward is that I believe we need a reboot when it comes to church planting. We simply need to wrench it out of its Fordist framework and re-imagine it within the growing framework of the Artisan Economy.

You see, there are many parallels between the changing global economy and church planting. As much as cities such as Detroit or Cleveland or Milwaukee or Pittsburgh might wish to reassert their status as world-class producers of steel and other manufactured products, that would be impossible. They have already seen the bulk of their jobs move either overseas or to the Sunbelt cities. Rather than hold onto their bygone status, it is imperative for them to aggressively move forward in a new direction. Even though there is some pushback among academics over the fact that Milwaukee is going all-in on wooing the creative class, what choice do they have? Globalization has shifted the geographic centers of economics and manufacturing. Time will tell if they will succeed or not and there are already signs of hope and change in cities like Cleveland and Detroit. They are rebounding.

Similarly, what I find today are denominations and church planting organizations and networks redoubling their efforts in hopes of regaining their former status as mass-producers of new one-size-fits-all church plants. Rather than yearning for what once was, what if instead they charted a new way forward in light of the changing economics of globalization? I believe that to do so would not only produce more churches, but they would also be more innovative and adaptable. Look again at the characteristics of the Artisan Economy in the above-referenced chart and imagine them being applied to church plants. [30] Here are several examples:

- *Similar but not uniform*—While there will always be universal elements of church throughout history and across cultures (similar), artisan churches will not be uniform as they are influenced by context and culture.
- *Variation is appreciated*—There is much variation not only between the churches, but even in how training is done and carried out. It is localized and contextual.
- *Improvisational*—Artisan churches adapt to context and the church planters themselves are improvisational.

---

[30] In introducing these concepts I am fully aware that I am not taking the time to delineate between church forms or expressions and theology. I am not advocating for jettisoning a historically developed theology, but instead for the need to continue to contextualize biblical truths to culture and learn to identify one's own cultural blind spots. For a good resource to walk through the contextualization process I would recommend *Center Church* by Timothy Keller.

- *Locally distinct*—Contextualized to each setting in the city, not only will urban churches differ from their suburban counterparts, but they will also vary from district to district and neighborhood to neighborhood in the same part of the city.
- *Work follows seasonal rhythms*—Church planting is more of a way of life than a job.
- *Less is more*—Artisan churches are streamlined and minimalistic.[31]
- *Clustered, collaborative firms*—Church planters embrace collaboration thus creating incubators for mission innovation.

A new era is upon us thanks to globalization. The creative or artisan economy in the West is shaping and reshaping our cities. It is time that we let it do the same for church planting in North America.

---

[31] This does not necessitate house churches nor downplay public worship gatherings.

Chapter 6

Walkable Urbanism and Creating Neighborhoods That Work

There are two facets of the city that influence my thinking and impact my personal life more than anything else: the built environment and transportation infrastructure. These two pieces of the city influence the day-to-day lives of billions of city dwellers more than we realize. Why is that? How is that?

Stop for a moment and think with me. What is your favorite city? What makes it your favorite city? Most often we think of cities we have visited and vacationed in whether at home or abroad. If you were to show me the pictures from your trip more than likely it would show you walking around some historic district with cobblestone streets and old buildings in the background as you sip on espresso, savor a bowl of gelato, or eat some of the local delicacies. Maybe your mind has a flashback to walking around The Bund in Shanghai, Old Montréal, Old Town in Portland, Gastown in Vancouver BC, and many other similar places. Most often such places are defined by their built environment which in turn influences how people get around.

A city's built environment and transportation infrastructure are intrinsically linked. They also shaped how the gathered church in the first century as well as how the Gospel spread. Our lives today, and that of the church, are still directly impacted, and in some ways determined, by a city's built environment and transportation infrastructure.

Before we proceed any further, we need to ask ourselves why we are all drawn towards certain cities and especially places in those cities that are historic and walkable. Last fall I spent a half-day by myself walking around Old Montréal. The stone buildings dating back to the 1600s, cobblestoned roadways, and narrow streets make it a desirable place to visit for residents and tourists alike. For hours I wandered the streets, stopping on occasion to sit on a bench. The beauty of the place and the power of its historicity were truly moving. At times I was almost in tears as I prayed for the people.

I am not the only one who's drawn to these kinds of places. For millions of tourists there is a sort of magnetic pull to Old Montréal. A touch of history indeed. The narrow walkable streets are a reminder of what our cities were once like. Maybe people have a deep longing to return to this kind of living as it stands in such stark contrast to our sprawling auto-centric cities filled with bland architecture.

During the latter half of the twentieth century, North American cities saw their populations being propelled outwards to the suburbs in an ever-widening radius, as if they had been caught up in a giant centrifuge. Awaiting them there were low-density single family detached homes. Cities went from being traditionally walkable and pedestrian-friendly in their central neighborhoods to being auto-dependent and sprawling on the urban periphery and in the suburbs. There is today a growing movement that seeks to counter-balance this, whether through the initiatives and influence of the Congress for the New Urbanism, retrofitting and urbanizing the suburbs, or generalized plans for such things as walkable districts and neighborhoods, tactical urbanism, creative architecture, and other thoughtful ways to create healthier cities and streetscapes.

This chapter looks into the differing dynamics that cities are utilizing to foster a more walkable urbanism. As we'll see, the missiological implications as well as the practical applications for the church are enormous. A walkable urbanism determines much of the daily and weekly rhythms of the church, and how and where people gather.

Cities across North America are involved in various type of urban regeneration projects, whether in the downtown core, other central city neighborhoods, or even the suburbs. One of the common elements in downtown revitalization plans, apart from reorienting their economic strategies to attract and retain the footloose creative class, is to create vibrant walkable urban neighborhoods and districts. Walkable urbanism is a key component to create specific urban amenities that appeal to these cultural creatives. These strategies are not limited to altering the built environment as a way to foster walkability, but they also involve other creative ways that cities, through projects both small and large, are attempting to chart a course for a new urban future.

For many, the reality of bland standardized suburban sprawl, which to be fair did provide home ownership opportunities for millions of Americans, is not the ideal future in terms of the built environment of the city. This is also buttressed by the changing attitudes and preferences of the American public, in particular the successive younger generations who are opting for an urban lifestyle rather than the suburban lifestyle they may grown up with.

Walkable Urbanism / Retrofitting Suburbia[1]

The Congress for the New Urbanism (CNU)[2] advocates for a decisive shift away from low-density auto-dependent suburban sprawl to reclaim a bit of America's past. One of their aims is to rekindle some of the vibrancy that characterized the central cities and small towns of yesterday, namely the neighborliness of a walkable community. "The Congress for the New Urbanism views disinvestment in central cities, the spread of placeless sprawl, increasing separation by race and income, environmental deterioration, loss of agricultural lands and wilderness, and the erosion of society's heritage as one interrelated community-building challenge."[3] This is a healthy and timely corrective measure as they seek to espouse and highlight certain elements of urban life that are appealing to a growing number of North Americans. This explains some of the popularity of places such

---

[1] Those familiar with my writings may recognize that on occasion I use examples or quotes from a couple of my other books. This is solely because what I am about to say I believe I've said better somewhere else. There are some similarities between this section and the section on Policy Recommendations in Chapter 5 of in my book *Blueprints for a Just City*.

[2] www.cnu.org.

[3] Congress for the New Urbanism, "Charter of the New Urbanism," 357.

as Old Montréal, Old Town in Portland, or even the Amana Colonies in Iowa.

What the CNU seeks to do is rectify the problems that rampant sprawl and thoughtless suburbanization have brought upon the American public. In addition, they view many aspects of low-density auto-based suburban life as hazardous to one's health. As Jeff Speck writes, "While battle was never declared, many American cities seem to have been made and remade with a mandate to defeat pedestrians. Fattened roads, emaciated sidewalks, deleted trees, fry-pit drive-thrus, and ten-acre parking lots have reduced many of our streetscapes to auto zones in which pedestrian life is but a theoretical possibility."[4] Speck and the CNU share much of the same angst in terms of not only the blandness and sterility of the suburbs, but also the need to create and recreate walkable neighborhoods and districts in cities whether urban or suburban.

For many, including Speck and the CNU, there is a yearning to what it was like to live in walkable cities and small towns. Eric Jacobsen writes, "The advantages that cities and traditional neighborhoods have over sprawling suburbs with respect to interdependence is that they allow people of a greater variety of ages to participate meaningfully in the culture."[5] Walkability then becomes more than mobility issues, but in fact broadens the scope of the conversation to include livable cities, cultural amenities, and what makes for the good life in the city ... and neighbors.

---

[4] Speck, *Walkable Cities*, 15.

[5] Jacobsen, *Sidewalks in the Kingdom*, 26.

Where this becomes important is that not only are the younger generations opting for an urban lifestyle, but by and large so is the creative class. Various studies have revealed this trend and researchers such as Richard Florida have been keen to highlight the importance of place. Not just *any* place, but cities, and not simply *any* city, but the ones that have a certain "Quality of Place." This points specifically to concepts of vibrant streetscapes and walkable urbanism.

> It [Quality of Place] refers to the unique set of characteristics that define a place and make it attractive. Generally, one can think of quality of place as having three dimensions: *What's there:* the combination of the built environment and the natural environment; a proper setting for pursuit of creative lives. *Who's there:* the diverse kinds of people, interacting and providing cues that anyone can plug into and make a life in that community. *What's going on:* the vibrancy of street life, café culture, arts, music and people engaging in outdoor activities—altogether a lot of active, exciting, creative endeavors.[6]

Ehrenhalt asks, "Where do the Millennials want to live? In many ways, this is the demographic question that will determine the face of metropolitan America in the next twenty years."[7] In his chapter on "Urbanizing the Suburbs," Ehrenhalt advocates that these urban amenities (including a walkable urbanism) be introduced in the suburbs as well as in the central city. As house prices and the cost of living in central cities escalate, places like Manhattan or the Loop in Chicago

---

[6] Florida, *The Rise of the Creative Class*, 232.

[7] Ehrenhalt, *The Great Inversion and the Future of the American City*, loc. 2990.

become inaccessible to Millennials who are just starting out. Instead, Ehrenhalt asserts that we need to create these same dynamics in the more affordable suburbs, and that the suburbs need to embrace a significantly higher-density built environment.

> The lesson is that if retrofitted suburbia is to meet the demands for classic urbanism that today's millennial generation tells so many polltakers it wants, suburban retrofits will have to become much, much denser. They will need to move beyond sidewalks cafés and nighttime street life and build buildings with enough tenants and homeowners to support the retail on the ground floor, without a six-lane highway whizzing by just a couple of blocks away. They will need to have transit stations integrated into the very fabric of the developments. Whether this is possible, I don't know. The suburban retrofits are, despite the number of examples that multiply every year, in only the earliest stages.[8]

However, the call for a walkable urbanism, including some of the CNU's basic tenets, has received pushback on numerous fronts. Where it breaks down is over what to focus on first: the buildings or the people (i.e., the culture). In terms of place-making, which is more important? Architect B.D. Wortham-Galvin reveals this tension in the competing advocacies of the CNU and Jane Jacobs. While both would claim that they are advocating for the same thing, it is the *how* or the starting point that is polemical. "The New Urbanists employ a tautological approach—that architecture should be based on architecture. In contrast, Jacobs's seminal tract, *The*

---

[8] Ibid., loc. 3168.

Death and Life of Great American Cities, makes the argument that architecture should start with culture in order to make place in the city."[9] For the CNU, the starting point is design or architecture. For Jacobs, according to Wortham-Galvin, the starting point is culture:

> It is hard for New Urbanism to foster Jacobs's beloved notions of diversity and vitality of uses, people, economies and ecologies when implementing the unifying vision of a comprehensive plan, instead of infilling tactically in an extant culture. When culture is, therefore, rendered homogenous and applied from the top down, organic transformation and the potential for democratic action are slighted and made invisible, if not impossible.[10]

Organic Urbanism

In contrast to the CNU's almost technocratic approach to urban planning and retrofitting, there is a growing movement of people "taking back their streets" and creating ad hoc forms of vibrant walkable urbanism. Rebecca Sanborn Stone writes about a "guerrilla urbanism," Benjamin de la Peña explains the importance of the "autocatalytic city," and Charles Wolfe pushes for an "urbanism without effort." In each case, the common denominator is a form of urbanism and place-making that is more "bottom-up" than the zoned and regulated approach used by developers and local governments. However, the desired outcomes of both are the same, to create

---

[9] Wortham-Galvin, "Making the Familiar Strange," 238.

[10] Ibid., 239.

vibrant walkable streetscapes that are enjoyable to live in and experience. They just go about it in different ways.

This is where the church can have a direct impact. Churches are not urban planners, but they can be about other activities that foster a   walkable vibrant urbanism. I will expand on later.

Rebecca Sanborn Stone in her chapter "Guerrilla Urbanism" in *City 2.0* writes about "tactical urbanism," which "uses short-term actions to catalyze real, long-term change. It might be quirky, but it's a serious strategy for creating more vibrant, livable places through lightweight, temporary, grassroots projects called interventions."[11] More than a hipster prank, these are ways that people across the planet are reclaiming spaces in cities and repurposing them. In some cases they are only temporary, but in others what starts off as temporary turns into permanent. These are cheap, creative, and flexible ways to improve urban life for city dwellers from pop-up or pocket parks to ad hoc movies in a vacant lot.

The goal is not simply to stage a show, but to organically create change in the urban fabric of the city. "Tactical urbanism offers a way to revitalize neighborhoods and build those more livable urban environments right now and with minimal red tape."[12]

In the *Tactical Urbanism* guidebook, Jaime Lerner, the architect and former mayor of Curitiba, Brazil, is quoting as saying "The lack of resources is no longer an excuse not to act. The idea that action should be taken after all the answers and

---

[11] Stone, "Guerrilla Urbanism," loc. 788.

[12] Ibid., loc. 799.

the resources have been found is a sure recipe for paralysis. The planning of a city is a process that allows for corrections; it is supremely arrogant to believe that planning can be done only after every possible variable has been controlled."[13] The city of Curitiba is an inspiration because it recreated its urbanism with little to no resources. Every time an issue arose, from traffic congestion to trash build-up in the slums, the mayor would say, "We need to fix this ... but we don't have any money." The lack of resources forced them to innovate in ways that created a model global city from reclaiming park space to its BRT[14] system.

The concept of tactical urbanism posits that there are creative and cost-efficient ways to create a vibrant walkable urbanism in cities. The guidebook sets out an alternative way to redevelop cities. Churches, take note:

> Improving the livability of our towns and cities commonly starts at the street, block, or building scale. While larger scale efforts do have their place, incremental, small-scale improvements are increasingly seen as a way to stage more substantial investments. This approach allows a host of local actors to test new concepts before making substantial political and financial commitments. Sometimes sanctioned, sometimes not, these actions are commonly referred to as "guerrilla urbanism," "pop-up urbanism," "city repair," or "D.I.Y. urbanism."[15]

---

[13] Lydon et al, *Tactical Urbanism*, iv.

[14] Bus Rapid Transit.

[15] *Tactical Urbanism*, 1.

There are a wide variety of creative ways that city dwellers can be engaged in improving the livability of their cities such as: Park(ing) Day,[16] food carts, informal bike parking,[17] pavement to plazas or parks,[18] reclaimed setbacks,[19] open streets,[20] micro-mixing,[21] and pop-up retail space[22] or cafes[23] to name a few. These are many ways that people can enliven and reclaim their neighborhoods and districts.

This approach also stimulates new ways of thinking that churches can actually be part of in making their cities livable, vibrant, and walkable. While to many, especially in the church, these are probably foreign concepts we need to think of these as ways to promote God-ordained human flourishing, which also creates better conditions for interconnectivity and

---

[16] "To reclaim space devoted to automobiles, and to increase the vitality of street life." Ibid., 15.

[17] "To increase the supply of bicycle parking where needed." Ibid., 30.

[18] "To reclaim underutilized asphalt as public space without large capital expenditure." Ibid., 19.

[19] "To create a more engaging streetscape by activating the space between the structure and the sidewalk." Ibid., 34.

[20] "To temporarily provide safe spaces for walking, bicycling, skating and social activities; promote local economic development; and raise awareness about the detrimental effects of the automobile on urban living." Ibid., 11.

[21] "To incubate new businesses and sustain existing ones through the co-location of mutually supportive uses." Ibid., 39.

[22] "To promote the temporary use of vacant retail space or lots." Ibid., 17.

[23] "To promote outdoor public seating in the parking lane (during the warm months) and to promote local businesses." Ibid., 21.

even ways for the Gospel to spread rapidly, non-programmatically, relationally, and organically.

Benjamin de la Peña writes about "the autocatalytic city." In this framework, he is advocating for more of a "messy urbanism" which stands in stark contrast to the CNU. Some of its critics say it should really be called the Congress for the New *Suburbanism* because what it proposes can only lead to homogeneity and even a certain level of blandness. A number of model new urbanist communities have been derided both for their ethnic homogeneity, and for being havens of the middle class and the wealthy.

The messy urbanism that Peña writes about is at the other end of the spectrum. Part of his approach is in how he views the city: "Urban centers are evolving organisms, not engineering problems."[24] In this he pushes for a bottom-up urbanism that "actually works for the people in them."[25] Peña adds:

> Our understanding of cities has been shaped by our Industrial Age expectations of institutional control. As urban centers boom around the globe, however, we are hitting the limits of the machine model of cities. Metropolises are growing too fast for our industrial models to work. Our task, as so ably argued by author and urban activist Jane Jacobs, is not to command the city but to understand the processes that make it work.[26]

---

[24] de la Peña, "The Autocatalytic City," loc. 965.

[25] Ibid., loc. 976.

[26] Ibid., loc. 1045.

Many examples of autocatalytic cities can be found in squatter developments on the urban periphery of cities in most of the developing countries. While at first glance these seem chaotic and disorganized, and in fact some are, what they reveal is a form of urbanism that we can learn from. Peeling back the layers, one finds innovation and entrepreneurialism as people, despite the odds stacked against them, figure out ways to not only survive but to thrive as best they can. One outcome is the creation of informal economies where people create, market, and sell their wares. Many of the urban districts that we enjoy today started off as more or less ad hoc developments without master plans. While these were different from squatter settlements, there was still an inherently autocatalytic nature to these places.

Urbanism Without Effort by Charles Wolfe is a book whose ethos is in sync with both Stone and Peña. Wolfe even pulls together the polar extremes of organic urbanism versus the CNU framework: "As the discussions continue today, the question of authentic versus prescribed urbanism should remain at the center of urban stakeholder dialogue."[27] Where his position is unique among the extreme polarities is in calling for the need to look beneath the surface of current urban realities. "While we might champion the programmed success of certain iconic examples, we risk ignoring the backstory of urban forms and functions, and failing to truly understand the traditional relationships between people and place."[28] Wolfe points to numerous cities and places that many of us love, enjoy, and adore, and shows that one of the reasons

---

[27] Wolfe, *Urbanism Without Effort*, loc. 97.

[28] Ibid., loc. 117.

...d their success and appeal was precisely because they ..w organically ... without effort.

Rachel Armstrong in her book *Living Architecture* gets at what Wolfe and others are advocating. Writing from the architectural or physical design perspective, she notes that our cities are more shaped by connectivity; there is a fluidity to them. "21st-century society draws from a world that is less determined by objects and increasingly shaped by connectivity."[29] Cities are less predetermined and mechanistic than we realize, but are in act more organic or autocatalytic. These are the processes that are changing and rearranging cities. She advocates moving away from the machine motif of cities and instead look at them as living, breathing organisms. "Unlike machines, living systems are native and positive contributors to the biosphere."[30] This framework allows for a flexibility in our urban environments. One of the ways in which this flexibility is being tested is with our homes. Kent Larson writes:

> Seventy percent of humanity will likely live in cities by 2050. A limited number of creative, vibrant cities, however, will dominate the cultural and economic life of the planet by actively nurturing entrepreneurship and attracting the young, technology-savvy professional who drive innovation and build new industries. But as demand relentlessly increases housing prices, the most desirable cities are becoming unaffordable for the very people whom they need to attract to remain globally competitive.[31]

---

[29] Armstrong, Living Architecture., loc. 149.

[30] Ibid., loc. 139.

[31] Larson, "Flex homes," loc. 881.

This gives rise to what Larson calls "flex homes" which are smaller but yet more efficient and innovative living spaces. In his chapter "Flex homes: The future of urban dwellings is tiny and transformable" in *City 2.0*, Larson seeks to rectify the problem of expensive housing:

> The answer to this problem lies not in building tiny conventional apartments but in creating hyper-efficient, technology-enabled spaces that transform dynamically to function as if much larger. It is entirely possible to build a 250-square-foot apartment with king-size bed, dining area for eight people, party space with 60-inch HDTV, fully equipped kitchen, and handicapped-accessible bathroom—but, of course, these functions are not all available simultaneously.[32]

At first glance this seems as preposterous as a bad futuristic sci-fi movie. However, cities are congested spaces and as more that people move into cities, the greater the premium is going to be placed on space. If we want to be able to house more people more affordably, then creativity and innovation are key.

The purpose of this journey through guerrilla urbanism, autocatalytic cites, urbanism without effort, and flex homes is to show that there are many creative ways to live and create vibrant cities. The gift of common grace is all around us as God works through people, most often those who would not identify themselves as a follower of Jesus, to create healthy, vibrant, and walkable cities. It is time for the church to ride the wave of this common grace and infuse it with saving grace.

---

[32] Ibid., loc. 891.

Can the Church Create Gospel-Centered Urbanism?

Here is a question truly worth considering: Can the church create Gospel-centered urbanism? Or should that be the role of individual Christians in their neighborhoods? The follow-up questions are also worth exploring: What is Gospel-centered urbanism? What do I mean by Gospel-centered? Is there such a thing? Can that label (the Gospel) be applied to urbanism? If we were to take up this challenge, do we run the risk of simply creating another subcultural experience like *Christian* music, *Christian* broadcasting, etc.? Lastly, what are the implications for church planters in the city?

Maybe you're like me and have grown weary of labels. I have been a part of the church long enough to have watched labels ebb and flow. Admittedly, each new label is usually a course correction that tries to draw the church back to its roots as a missional community. (Oops, I just used a label). Whether *emerging, missional, or Gospel-centered*, these labels started off as powerful reminders of key biblical truths. This is healthy and necessary to get our attention.

Albert Gilbert wrote an article for the *International Journal of Urban and Regional Research* entitled, "The Return of Slum: Does Language Matter?" Gilbert questions the UN for reintroducing the term in 1999 with its "Cities Without Slums" initiative. Is the term helpful, or did the UN reintroduce it simply because of its shock value? In a world with competing media interests, does "slum" generate a bigger buzz? Gilbert argues that while it certainly may stir up more public interest, there could be a downside in equating the negative attributes of a "slum" with those living there. Can slum-like qualities be separated from slum-dwellers? "What makes the word 'slum' dangerous is the series of negative associations that the term conjures up, the false hopes that a campaign against slums raises and the mischief that unscrupulous politicians, developers and planners may do with the term."[33]

The two major outcomes that result from using the term are the devaluation of *places* and the devaluation of *people*.[34] When one or the other (or both) are devalued then it becomes easier for governments to become callous in their treatment of these places and people. If something is labeled a "slum" then one of the solutions becomes "slum removal." When people are devalued as "slum-dwellers" then it becomes easier to displace them.

Gilbert's article is helpful because it forces the reader to think through the meaning and usage of the term "slum." Words and labels are powerful and need to be used wisely.

The last few years have seen an uptick in all-things *Gospel-centered*. Again, this is a healthy corrective, but after a while it like many other labels can be applied so broadly and generically that *everything* becomes *emerging*, *everything* becomes *missional*, and *everything* becomes *Gospel-centered*. We cannot simply have a small group, it has to be a *Gospel-centered* small group. The problem is not with the words but in

---

[33] Gilbert, "The Return of the Slum," 701.

[34] Ibid., 702-703.

our overuse (and misuse) of them to the point where they lose their potency, and thus create the need for another label.

So can we create a *Gospel-centered* urbanism? Am I running the risk of simply dressing up urbanism with the latest label? To a degree, yes, but I think if unpacked correctly, *Gospel-centered* works here. As I have articulated at length in other books such as *Blueprints for a Just City* and *The Urbanity of the Bible*, the scope and implications of the Gospel are far-reaching. It moves beyond simply rescuing souls for heaven and in the process leaving the earth and its physical space as a wasteland. Instead, the full scope of the Gospel as the good news that the Kingdom of Heaven is at hand, is to seek to redeem both *people* and *places*. As such, "Gospel-centered" provides the right kind of descriptor when attached to *urbanism*.

If we believe that God created cities for human flourishing, then when we lean into that calling,[35] we are doing precisely what God commanded humanity to do from the beginning. In other words, to advocate for and help create healthy, vibrant, walkable neighborhoods, districts, and cities is indeed Gospel-centered because we are Christ's conduits of both common and saving grace to our cities. The Gospel is that Jesus died for the sins of Adam which had devastated the world and the hope of human flourishing, as well as for our sins which have devastated our own lives, our families, our neighborhoods, and our cities as well as the natural environment. The Gospel of Jesus came to redeem us of our brokenness and the resultant impact upon creation. While the

---

[35] See the urban mandate in Genesis 1:28.

152

fulness or climax of redemption will not be fully realized until the end, when we go about sharing the Gospel with people as well as living out its implications in our cities we are promoting human flourishing. This I would contend reaches its fullest meaning when it is truly Gospel-centered.

While we aim to see the flourishing of our cities, whether through a vibrant economy or in small ways like tactical urbanism, the greatest depth of this flourishing can only be found in the Gospel. The church's direct involvement is most often not required for our cities to become healthy and vibrant, in terms of their economy, an activated urbanism, equity, or growth of the arts. However, that does not negate for a moment that God is truly the architect behind it all through his providence and common grace. As R.C. Sproul says "it is appropriate to use the word *providence* with reference to God's active governance of the universe."[36]

There have been many cases where the church really was instrumental in transforming society. But I believe the most potent form of urbanism is this notion of *Gospel-centered urbanism*, where human flourishing in our cities, including the built environment, is promoted in conjunction with modeling and sharing the Gospel. Without Gospel proclamation we will see the effects of God's common grace as set out in Romans 1:19-21, but that is not enough to save or redeem. It needs to be coupled with saving grace.

---

[36] Sproul, *Does God Control Everything?*, loc. 125.

Pedestrian-Oriented Church Planting

The more we see such things as guerrilla or tactical urbanism initiatives crop up, the more I believe traction develops for the furtherance of the Gospel, both in word and deed. When we trek through the dusty streets and alleyways of First Century cities we watch and note how the Gospel spread. To say that the church in the New Testament was walkable would be an understatement. What it reveals is that there can be explosive growth and movement without the aid of all the technology that we have today. That does not mean technology is wrong or ought not to be utilized, quite the opposite. The point is that the Gospel spreads fastest through dense relational lines. When cities, whether large scale or at the bottom-up grassroots level, push for a more vibrant walkable urbanism, inevitably it densifies possible relational connections.

I have previously written in multiple places about the need to reorient church planting around a walkable[37] or bikeable[38] scale. For too long, despite changing transportation usage, most church planting and church growth techniques have focused on auto-centric commuting patterns. Churches are encouraged to be regional churches where the congregation drives in from all over the metro area and then after the worship service are flung back out like a centrifuge. Churches

---

[37] *The Multi-Nucleated Church: Towards a Theoretical Framework for Church Planting in High-Density Cities.* Portland: Urban Loft, 2015.

[38] *The Bikeable Church: A Bicyclist's Guide to Church Planting.* Portland, Urban Loft, 2015.

are encouraged to have ample parking spaces if they want to grow. On some levels this is still good missiology as it is cognizant of the current cultural norms of North American cities. But as cities become more walkable and bikeable what is needed are alternatives to this approach in church planting. What is needed is pedestrian-oriented church planting.

In *View From the Urban Loft* I introduced this concept. "Pedestrian-Oriented Church Planting is starting walkable churches in dense neighborhoods that are accessible by foot, available for all local inhabitants (rich, poor, young, old, and different ethnicities), rooted in the community, and acts as lead catalysts in community transformation."[39] This meshes with the concepts of guerrilla or tactical urbanism, the autocatalytic city, and urbanism without effort. In city neighborhoods and districts that are densifying and working to create a sense of vibrant walkable urbanism, this mode of church planting needs to at least be considered.

City after city across North America are moving in this direction. This is not merely a phenomenon in New York City, Portland, or San Francisco, but cities like Asheville, Wichita, Boise, or Waco are also moving into this direction. Cities have collectively bought into creative class strategies and are using them to rebuild their urban fabric in order to woo people back into their downtowns. The big selling points are loft living, walkable urbanism, bikeability, and cultural and entertainment amenities. Certainly, if churches move towards thinking and acting like missionaries as well as developing a missiological framework through which to operate, then that

---

[39] Benesh. *View From the Urban Loft*, 165.

means in neighborhoods and districts where this shift has occurred we should adapt accordingly.

The potency behind pedestrian-oriented church planting is that it aligns with the trajectory in which cities are going. If certain cities are reducing parking to foster walkability and bikeability then the notion of auto-oriented regional churches needs to be readdressed in those settings. Our purpose should not be to plant churches that are novel, but instead to think and act like missionaries. As we watch cities, through God's providence and common grace, move towards being more sustainable and less dependent upon the auto, then the church should at least consider in that same direction as well.

Afterword

As I look back on the topics covered in this book I fully understand that they represent only a fraction of the trends that are shaping and reshaping North American cities. I realize too that I only dove into those topics relating mostly to the built environment, whether urban renewal projects, suburbanization, walkability, and so on. Even the conversion to a Post-Fordist economy has direct ramifications on the built environment. As I pedal my bike through various neighborhoods that are either going through rapid gentrification or are on the receiving end of a massive influx of young creatives (or both), inevitably it coincides with a densifying streetscape as four- to five-story mixed-use apartments are being constructed along these narrow corridors. There is an economic engine behind this.

In other words, there are more topics that I did not address that need to be addressed, but that is for other books and other authors. These topics are simply the ones in my wheelhouse that I'm most interested in and passionate about. I am visual. I agree with Sam Bass Warner and Andrew

Whittemore: "Studying a city is first of all a visual sport."[1] They make the case that understanding the built environment of a city not only unlocks its past but helps us set the course for the future as well. "If one understands that the transportation patterns and ways of doing business in a city have been altered over time, as indeed they have often been in the past, then the previous geographies of a city emerge. With such insights the citizen is in a position to consider what aspects of urban life he or she would like to maintain and what others to change."[2]

There are numerous ways that the church can impact and influence the city. It is my contention that an often overlooked component is that of the built environment. As we traversed through history in these pages we have seen how changing urban forms influenced the life and lifestyle of Americans. There is a power in the built environment. As Winston Churchill once said, "We shape our buildings; thereafter they shape us." But what would things look like if the church helped shape the city? What if the church helped advocate for a more equitable urban form?

For you the church planter ... does any of this impact or influence how you will go about planting a church in the city?

---

[1] Warner and Whittemore, *American Urban Form*, 3.

[2] Ibid., 4.

Bibliography

Adler, Sy, and Johanna Brenner. "Gender and Space: Lesbians
    and Gay Men in the City." In *The Urban Sociology
    Reader*, edited by Jan Lin and Christopher Mele,
    200-207. New York: Routledge, 2012.

Armstrong, Rachel. *Living Architecture: How Synthetic Biology
    Can Remake Our Cities and Reshape Our Lives*. New
    York: TED Books, 2012. Kindle edition.

Benesh, Sean. *Metrospiritual: The Geography of Church
    Planting*. Eugene: Resource, 2011.

_____. *View From the Urban Loft: Developing a Theological
    Framework for Understanding the City*. Eugene:
    Resource, 2011.

Bosch, David J. *Transforming Mission: Paradigm Shifts in
    Theology of Mission*. Maryknoll: Orbis, 1991.

Bruegmann, Robert. "The Cause of Sprawl." In *The City
    Reader*, edited by Richard T. LeGates and Frederic
    Stout, 211-221. New York: Routledge, 2011.

Burayidi, Michael A. *Downtowns: Revitalizing the Centers of
    Small Urban Communities*. New York: Routledge,
    2001.

Butler, Tim. "Consumption and Culture." In *The Gentrification
    Debates: A Reader*, edited by Japonica Brown-
    Saracino, 235-260. New York, Routledge, 2010.

Carmon, Naomi. "Three generations of urban renewal policies:
    analysis and policy implications." *Geoforum* 3 (1999)
    145-158.

Case Western Reserve University. "Moving to the City? Join the Crowd." No pages. Online: http://case.edu/magazine/fallwinter2012/discover/moving.html.

Chapin, Timothy S. "Sports Facilities as Urban Redevelopment Catalysts: Baltimore's Camden Yards and Cleveland's Gateway." *Journal of the American Planning Association* 70:2 (2004) 193-209.

CNN.com. "High school gym roof collapses in Cleveland." No pages. Online: http://archives.cnn.com/2000/US/10/06/school.collapse.01/.

Congress for the New Urbanism. "Charter of the New Urbanism." In *The City Reader*, edited by Richard T. LeGates and Frederic Stout, 356-359. 5th ed. New York: Routledge, 2011.

Currid, Elizabeth. "How Art and Culture Happen in New York." *Journal of American Planning Association* 73:4 (2007) 454-467.

del la Peña, Benjamin. "The Autocatalytic City." In *City 2.0: The Habitat of the Future and How to Get There*. New York: TED Books, 2012. Kindle edition.

Dictionary.com, Inc. "Enculturation." Dictionary.com. Online: http://dictionary.reference.com/browse/enculturation?s=t.

Donegan, Mary, et al. "Which Indicators Explain Metropolitan Economic Performance Best?" *Journal of the American Planning Association* 74:2 (2008) 180-195.

Dunham-Jones, Ellen, and June Williamson. *Retrofitting Suburbia: Urban Design Solutions for Redesigning Suburbs*. Hoboken: John Wiley & Sons, 2011.

Dunham-Jones, Ellen. "Next Generation Urbanism." Lecture presented at Simon Fraser University, Vancouver, British Columbia, October 26, 2010.

Ehrenhalt, Alan. *The Great Inversion and the Future of the American City*. New York: Vintage, 2013.

Flanagan, William G. *Urban Sociology: Images and Structure*. 5th ed. Lanham: Rowman & Littlefield, 2010.

Florida, Richard. *Rise of the Creative Class: And How It's Transforming Work, Leisure, Community and Everyday Life.* New York: Basic, 2002.

_____. *The Great Reset: How New Ways of Living and Working Drive Post-Crash Prosperity.* New York: HarperCollins, 2010.

_____. "To Build Creative Cities, the Sky Has Its Limits." *The Wall Street Journal,* July 27, 2012. No pages. Online: http://online.wsj.com/article/ SB10000872396390443477104577551133804551396.html.

_____. "Detroit Shows Way to Beat Inner City Blues." *Financial Times,* April 9, 2013. no pages. Online: http://www.ft.com/intl/cms/s/ 0/7c1692b6-9c71-11e2-ba3c-00144feabdc0.html.

Fogelson, Robert M. *Downtown: Its Rise and Fall, 1880-1950.* New Haven: Yale University Press, 2001.

Freeman, Lance. "Displacement or Succession? Residential Mobility in Gentrifying Neighborhoods." *Urban Affairs Reviews* 40:4 (2005) 463-491.

Frost, Michael. *Exiles: Living Missionally in a Post-Christian Culture.* Grand Rapids: Baker, 2006.

_____, and Alan Hirsch. *The Shaping of Things to Come: Innovation and Mission for the 21 Century Church.* Peabody: Hendrickson, 2003.

Gilbert, Alan. "The Return of the Slum: Does Language Matter?" *International Journal of Urban and Regional Research* 31:4 (2007) 697–713.

Glaeser, Edward L. *Triumph of the City: How Our Greatest Invention Makes Us Richer, Smarter, Greener, Healthier, and Happier.* New York: Penguin, 2011.

Glass, Ruth. "Aspects of Change." In *The Gentrification Debates: A Reader,* edited by Japonica Brown-Saracino, 19-29. New York, Routledge, 2010.

Gordon, Colin. *Mapping Decline: St. Louis and the Fate of the American City.* Philadelphia: University of Pennsylvania Press, 2008.

Gordon, Wayne. "Gentrification: The Good News and the Bad News." In *A Heart for the Community: New Models for Urban and Suburban Ministry*, edited by John Fuder and Noel Castellanos, 39-49. Chicago: Moody, 2009.

Gottdiener, Mark, and Ray Hutchinson. *The New Urban Sociology*. 4th ed. Boulder: Westview, 2010.

Greenwald, Richard. "The Lifecycle of a 'Cool' Neighborhood." *The Atlantic Cities*, September 17, 2012. No pages. Online: http://www.theatlanticcities.com/arts-and-lifestyle/2012/09/lifecycle-cool-neighborhood/3280/.

Harvey, David. "The Right to the City." *International Journal of Urban and Regional Research*, 27:4 (2003) 939-941.

Heying, Charles. *Brew to Bikes: Portland's Artisan Economy*. Portland: Ooligan, 2010.

Hiller, Harry H. *Urban Canada*. 2nd ed. New York: Oxford University Press, 2009.

Historic Gateway Neighborhood Corporation + Gateway District, "Live." No pages. Online: http://www.clevelandgatewaydistrict.com/live/.

Hoyt, Lorlene M. "Do Business Improvement District Organizations Make a Difference?: Crime In and Around Commercial Areas in Philadelphia." *Journal of Planning Education and Research* 25 (2005) 185-199.

Hymowitz, Kay S. "How Brooklyn Got Its Groove Back." *City Journal*. 21:4(2011). No pages. Online: http://www.city-journal.org/2011/21_4_brooklyn.html.

Jacobsen, Eric O. *Sidewalks in the Kingdom: New Urbanism and the Christian Faith*. Grand Rapids: Brazos, 2003.

Jenkins, Philip. *The Next Christendom: The Coming of Global Christianity*. 2nd ed. New York: Oxford University Press, 2007.

Kotkin, Joel. "The Hollow Boom of Brooklyn: Behind Veneer of Gentrification, Life Gets Worse for Many." *Forbes*, September 25, 2012. No pages. Online:

http://www.forbes.com/sites/joelkotkin/2012/09/25/
the-hollow-boom-of-brooklyn-behind-veneer-of-
gentrification-life-gets-worse-for-many/.

Larson, Kent. "Flex homes." In *City 2.0: The Habitat of the
Future and How to Get There*. New York: TED
Books, 2012. Kindle edition.

Lee, Michael. "LeBron James will leave Cleveland Cavaliers to
join Dwayne Wade, Chris Bosh with Miami Heat."
Washington Post. No pages. Online: http://
www.washingtonpost.com/wp-dyn/content/article/
2010/07/08/AR2010070806865.html.

Lees, Loretta. "The Ambivalence of Diversity and the Politics
of Urban Renaissance: The Case of Youth in
Downtown Portland, Maine." *International Journal of
Urban and Regional Research* 27:3 (2003) 613-34.

Lees, Loretta, et al. *Gentrification*. New York: Routledge,
2007.

LeGates, Richard T., and Frederic Stout. *The City Reader*. 5th
ed. New York: Routledge, 2011.

Lind, Diana. "Cities Without Highways." In *City 2.0: The
Habitat of the Future and How to Get There*. New
York: TED Books, 2012. Kindle edition.

Lloyd, Richard. *Neo-Bohemia: Art and Commerce in the
Postindustrial City*. 2nd ed. New York: Routledge,
2010.

Lydon, Mike, et al. *Tactical Urbanism 2: Short Term Action,
Long-Term Change*. Miami: Street Plans, 2012.

Mapes, Jeff. *Pedaling Revolution: How Cyclists Are Changing
American Cities*. Corvallis: Oregon State University
Press, 2009.

Markusen, Ann. "Urban Development and the Politics of a
Creative Class: evidence from a study of artists."
Environment and Planning A 38 (2006) 1921-1940.

Maus, Jonathan. "Daimler Trucks North America opens new
bike parking facility on Swan Island."
BikePortland.org, April 30, 2013. Online: http://
bikeportland.org/2013/04/30/daimler-trucks-north-

america-cuts-ribbon-on-new-bike-parking-
facility-86146.

McCrary, Larry, et al. *Tradecraft: For the Church on Mission*.
Portland: Urban Loft, 2013.

Miller, Emily. "Pushing City Limits." *Relevant Magazine* 63
(2013). Online: http://www.relevantmagazine.com/
reject-apathy/pushing-city-limits-0.

Nicolaides, Becky M., and Andrew Wiese. "Suburban
Disequilibrium." *New York Times,* April 6, 2013. No
pages. Online: http://opinionator.blogs.nytimes.com/
2013/04/06/suburban-disequilibrium/?_r=0.

Nordahl, Darrin. *Making Transit Fun: How to Entice Motorists
from the Cars (and onto their feet, a bike, or bus)*.
Washington DC: Island, 2012. Kindle edition.

Phillips, E. Barbara. *City Lights: Urban-Suburban Life in the
Global Society*. 3rd ed. New York: Oxford University
Press, 2009.

Porter, Michael. "The Competitive Advantages of the Inner
City." In *The City Reader*, edited by Richard T.
LeGates and Frederic Stout, 282-295. 5th ed. New
York: Routledge, 2011.

Portland State University Senior Capstone, "Historical
Highlights of Hollywood." No pages. Online: http://
hollywood.pdx.edu.

Shenk, Wilbert R. "Foreword." In *Globalizing Theology: Belief
and Practice in an Era of World Christianity*, edited by
Craig Ott and Harold A. Netland, 9-11. Grand
Rapids: Baker Academic, 2006.

Slater, Tom. "Gentrification of the City." In *The New
Blackwell Companion to the City*, edited by Gary
Bridge and Sophie Watson, 571-585. 2nd ed.
Maldan: John Wiley & Sons, 2013.

Smith, Andrew. *Events and Urban Regeneration: The Strategic
Use of Events to Revitalise Cities*. New York:
Routledge, 2012.

Speck, Jeff. *Walkable City: How Downtown Can Save America, One Step at a Time*. New York: Farrar, Straus and Giroux, 2012.

Sproul, R.C. *Can I Know God's Will?* Lake Mary: Reformation Trust, 2009.

Stetzer, Ed. *Planting Missional Churches*. Nashville: B&H Academic, 2006.

Stone, Rebecca Sanborn. "Guerrilla Urbanism." In *City 2.0: The Habitat of the Future and How to Get There*. New York: TED Books, 2012. Kindle edition.

Sustain Southern Maine, "Portland: India Street neighborhood." No pages. Online: http://sustainsouthernmaine.org/pilot-communities/portlandindiast/.

Tacket, Matt. "South Auditorium Urban Renewal." No pages. Online: http://urbanhomespdx.com/2010/10/15/south-auditorium-urban-renewal/.

Toderian, Brent. "Moving on From Gentrification to 'Shared Neighborhoods.'" *Huffpost British Columbia*, May 21, 2013. No pages. Online: http://www.huffingtonpost.ca/brent-toderian/gentrification-shared-neighbourhoods_b_3315364.html.

UN-HABITAT. *Planning Sustainable Cities: Global Report on Human Settlements 2009*. London: Earthscan, 2009.

Uhalley, Stephen Jr., and Xiaoxin Wu. *China and Christianity:Burdened Past, Hopeful Future*. New York: Routledge, 2001.

von Hoffman, Alexander. *House by House, Block by Block: The Rebirth of America's Urban Neighborhoods*. New York: Oxford University Press, 2003.

Vanhoozer, Kevin J. "One Rule to Rule Them All?" In *Globalizing Theology: Belief and Practice in an Era of World Christianity*, edited by Craig Ott and Harold A. Netland, 85-126. Grand Rapids: Baker Academic, 2006.

Warner, Sam Bass, and Andrew H. Whittemore. *American Urban Form: A Representative History.* Cambridge: The MIT Press, 2013.

Wikimedia Foundation Inc. "Post-Fordism." *Wikipedia.* No pages. Online: https://en.wikipedia.org/wiki/Post-Fordism.

Wolfe, Charles R. *Urbanism Without Effort.* Washington DC: Island, 2013. Kindle edition.

Wortham-Galvin, B.D. "Making the Familiar Strange: Understanding Design as Cultural Practice." In *The Urban Wisdom of Jane Jacobs*, edited by Sonia Hart and Diane Zahm, 229-244. New York: Routledge, 2012.

Zimmerman, Jeffrey. "From brew town to cool town: Neoliberalism and the creative city development strategy in Milwaukee." *Cities* 25 (2008) 230-242.

Zukin, Sharon. "The Creation of a 'Loft Lifestyle." In *The Gentrification Debates: A Reader*, edited by Japonica Brown-Saracino, 175-184. New York, Routledge, 2010.

_____. *Naked City: The Death and Life of Authentic Urban Places.* New York: Oxford University Press, 2011.

_____. "Whose Culture? Whose City?" In *The Urban Sociology Reader*, edited by Jan Lin and Christopher Mele, 281-289. New York: Routledge, 2012.

About the Author

Coffee and bicycles define Sean's urban existence who believes the best way for exploring cities is on the seat of a bicycle as well as hanging out in third wave coffee shops. Sean is an urban missiologist who works in a creative partnership between TEAM as the Developer of Urban Strategy and Training and the Upstream Collective leading the PDX Loft.

www.seanbenesh.net

About Urban Loft Publishers

Urban Loft Publishers focuses on ideas, topics, themes, and conversations about all things urban. Renewing the city is the central theme and focus of what we publish. It is our intention to blend urban ministry, theology, urban planning, architecture, urbanism, stories, and the social sciences, as ways to drive the conversation. While we lean towards scholarly and academic works, we explore the fun and lighter sides of cities as well. We publish a wide variety of urban perspectives, from books by the experts about the city to personal stories and personal accounts of urbanites who live in the city.

www.urbanloftpublishers.com
@theurbanloft

Made in the USA
Lexington, KY
30 July 2016